Becoming a Person of Prayer

CHRIS CRAIG

Chris Craig

Mark 11:24

XULON PRESS

Dedication

I want to dedicate this book to three people. The first is to my wife, who is my best supporter, fan, and helpmate. Cindy, you make me better, and you have made my life much better!

I also want to dedicate this book to Dr. and Mrs. Ben Haley. Without their help this book would have never been published. Ben and Sue were the ones that made this dream a reality.

To all three of these people I owe much gratitude.

Acknowledgments

I have many people to thank for their help with this book. As I mentioned in the dedication, this work would not have been possible without the support of my wife and Ben and Sue Haley. My personal assistants at work, Brenda Martin and Lindsey Lee, helped me with the proofreading and many of the fine details to make this book happen. I also want to thank Andrea Phillips for her proofing the manuscript and giving many helpful tips.

Anything of much value usually has the help of several hands. I hope this book will add value to the spiritual lives of others. If it does, it is certainly because of the help these people gave me.

CONTENTS

PREFACE

W hy another book about prayer? There are so many already out there, why should a new one be written and much less read?

Well, it is my belief that prayer is one of the greatest things God has made available to us. I also believe it is greatly underused and certainly misunderstood by many people. In this book we will look at what the Bible clearly teaches about prayer and how to apply that to our lives. We will see that becoming a person of prayer is what Jesus intended for every Christian. We will also see how becoming a person of prayer will change your life and your world.

I hope God will use this book to help you become the praying person that Jesus was and that God intended for you to be!

1

HOW DO I PRAY

E arly in my ministry I was asked about prayer, and I remember what the person said to me. "Chris, I have been a Christian almost twenty years. I have been active in church my whole life, but I really do not know how to pray." She continued, "I have had preachers and Sunday School teachers and youth leaders tell me to pray, but I don't know how to pray. How do *you* pray?" I will never forget that conversation.

About ten years ago, a religious survey done in America asked people who were professing Christians, "Are you really satisfied that you are connecting with God and that things are happening when you pray?" Only twenty-five percent of the people said they were satisfied with their prayer life. I believe that probably is true in most churches and that it has been true for a long time.

"One day Jesus was praying in a certain place. When he had finished, one of the disciples said to him, 'Lord, teach us to pray, just as John taught his disciples' " (Luke 11:1). The desire to pray and to know how to pray effectively has been sought after for many, many years.

I want us to see what God has to say about this subject for us to gain a better understanding of prayer and to develop a better practice of prayer.

CONSTANTLY LEARN HOW TO PRAY

Prayer is essential to our lives as Christians. We must constantly be learning how to pray. It does not matter how religious we may be, how long we have been in church, or how much we have read about prayer. Prayer is about practicing praying; it is about connecting with God.

The men who walked and talked with Jesus requested, "Jesus, teach us how to pray." They understood that prayer is something we will never master. If we are serious about God and serious about connecting with God, a cry of our hearts or a desire of our lives never needs to be "I've graduated from the school of prayer" but "God, help me constantly be better at praying."

Prayer Is Vital

Prayer is so vital. Prayer is vital to who you are as a Christian, who I am as a Christian, and who we are in the church. Although I think we believe that intellectually, sometimes it does not sink from our head to our heart.

I remember a cartoon in a magazine that showed in sequences the pastor's secretary walking into his office and the old, bald, and chubby pastor on his knees praying. The secretary says, "Oh good, he's not busy." That was cute, but too often it might be true that if you were to ask, "What is the minister doing?" the response may be, "Go ahead and interrupt him." Or to, "What is my husband or wife doing?" someone may answer, "Oh, nothing important. We can get them." They may say, "That's a good thing to do." Praying is not just something to do. It is a vital part of our life.

Luke is sometimes called the gospel of prayer, and in Luke's revelation of Jesus Christ he talks about prayer and shows us Jesus Christ was a man of prayer. When Jesus was on earth, He was a hundred percent God and a hundred percent man. Jesus Christ on earth as God and man needed to pray. Prayer was a vital part of His life, His ministry, and His service. And we should be able to say, "If Jesus needed to pray, how much more we need to pray."

Luke 5:16 says, "But Jesus often withdrew to lonely places and prayed." He withdrew not to read the latest book, to study the great theological writers of His time, or even to study Scripture. He withdrew to pray. Jesus was a man of prayer and if Jesus needed to pray, how much more do I need to pray! How much we all need to.

Prayer is about a relationship with God. Prayer is about a relationship I hope you already have with God, and prayer is about maintaining and developing it. How many of your relationships will be strong if you never talk with that person or if you never listen to that person?

Our relationship with Jesus is the same. The more we talk to Him in prayer and the more we listen to Him, the more we develop that relationship with Him. Prayer is vital to our relationship to Christ just as it was vital for Christ's relationship with the Father.

PRAYER IS THE SOURCE OF POWER

Prayer is the source of power. There is power in prayer. John Knox was a Christian leader in the 1500s in Scotland. The Queen of England at that time was a mean and vicious woman but she said, "I fear John Knox on his knees praying more than I do the foreign enemy." She was not a godly ruler but she knew that when John Knox prayed, things happened. The power of prayer was not limited just to John Knox or to some Old Testament character. It is available for you and me, too.

Ed Young, Sr., went to Houston in the eighties to pastor the Second Baptist Church. At the time, four or five hundred people attended regularly. Now, the church averages thousands in worship on weekends.

When asked, "What is the key to your growth?" Young said a fundamental key is prayer. He said prayer is vital to their preaching, their visitation, their Bible study times, and to all they do. He stated clearly that their great success as a church is tied into prayer. The same God that has blessed their church can bless our churches, too.

J. Edgar Hoover was Director of the FBI from 1924 to 1972. Hoover was at times a questionable character, not known for great spirituality, but he said something I think is interesting. He said,

"Prayer is the greatest power there is. It is more powerful than any man, than any leader, than the atomic bomb." Hoover knew prayer connected people with God and there was nothing more powerful than God.

I love a statement from R. A. Torrey that certainly is worth remembering. What can prayer do? Torrey said prayer "can accomplish anything God Himself can accomplish."[1]

God can accomplish anything. When you are on your knees or when you are standing or you are driving and you are praying, what can you accomplish? You can accomplish anything God can accomplish, and God can accomplish everything. That is the power of prayer.

Jesus' followers said, "Lord, teach us to pray just as John taught his disciples." The disciples lived with Jesus. They were with Him all the time. They saw that often He would go away to pray. He would get up early. He would go away from them. He would stay up late and pray. They began to see prayer was the practice of His life. They began to see a connection between the power of Christ and His prayer life, so they said, "Jesus, teach us to pray."

And isn't it neat they said, "Teach us to pray like John taught his disciples"? What a great thing to say about John the Baptist—he taught his people to pray. One thing the Jewish rabbis in Jesus' day were known for is for teaching their people to pray. We should make a commitment to learn how to pray, and it needs to be a lifetime pursuit.

I read a story several years ago about a man who loved to pray. He loved to pray and spent long hours in prayer, and he wondered if it were just a personality thing. He discovered a book that talked about prayer and one's temperament and about how your personal temperament affects your prayer life. It claimed some people are bent to pray and some are not bent to pray. Let me tell you, please, never read that book because that is not true.

God did not make some people to pray and some not to pray. The Bible does not say you may have the psychological temperament to be a man of prayer and your friend may not. It does not say if he just wants to sing and you want to pray, that is fine with God. Jesus Christ left us the perfect example as a man of prayer. Prayer is for everyone. All of us can be great men and women of prayer, and we ought to seek to learn how to do this.

"Teach us to pray as John taught his disciples." This is not about my saying you do not know how to pray, let me teach you, but together let's learn more about prayer. Preachers have motivated people by telling them to go win the world, but motivation without education leads to frustration. They say, "Pray, pray, pray," but don't tell you how. I want us to be motivated to pray and to know how to pray, and I think that is what Jesus wants us to do.

There is a beautiful book by Andrew Murray. The title of it is *With Christ in the School of Prayer.*[2] Our life commitment ought to be, "Jesus, I want to be with You in the school of prayer." We will never graduate; we will never earn a degree. But when we get to heaven, if we have applied ourselves properly to this, there we will have our reward.

Why should we learn to pray? We should learn to pray because prayer is vital and prayer is powerful. We need to give our lives to working out and developing our prayer life.

KEY PERSONAL ISSUES IN PRAYER

Some personal issues are key to our prayer life, some things we need to be and some things we need to do.

PRAY

A key personal issue in developing your prayer life is that you pray. The first thing you need to do is simply to do it. The disciples did not say, "Lord, just teach us *about* prayer." They said, "Lord, teach us to pray. Lord, teach us to actually do it." We talk about prayer, we preach about prayer, we study about prayer, but really praying is a different matter, isn't it? Yes, I believe it is.

Dr. T. W. Hunt, a professor at Southwestern Seminary for years, is a wonderful man who later went to work for the Southern Baptist Convention in the area of prayer and spiritual development. Dr. Hunt asked pastors throughout America how much they prayed daily. I thought: these are pastors; they will do well in this area. Surely, it will be one or two hours a day. But when Dr. Hunt did this survey, the average length of time the pastors were in prayer was seven minutes a day. You know, for a pastor that is bad. That is not much time on your knees before Jesus Christ.

The first thing we need to do, as simple as it sounds, is we need to pray. We need to make a commitment not just to read about it, to hear about it, or to talk about it, but to do it. Remember, the hay never gets put into the barn by discussing it only. Yes, you need to discuss how to get the hay in the barn. Sometimes a committee can help you figure out how to get the hay in the barn, but eventually you have to get someone who will just put the hay in the barn. The same thing is true with prayer. Eventually, we just need to pray. We need to do it.

HUMILITY

A second key to prayer is humility. Jesus said,

When you pray say: "Father, hallowed be your name, your kingdom come. Give us each day our daily bread. Forgive us our sins, for we also forgive everyone who sins against us. And lead us not into temptation."

Luke 11:2-4

Matthew records these same words of Jesus in what we know as the Lord's Prayer (Matt. 6:9-13).

It seems something of a contradiction that we are told we can come before God boldly. We have access to God, but that does not mean we strut into His presence. It means we can come to Him, but we need to come to God humbly. Jesus is my best friend, but He is also my king. These are two things we need never forget.

Second Chronicles 7:14 is a classic verse that says, "If my people, who are called by my name, will humble themselves and pray...." Remember, as we approach God in prayer, humility is a very important thing.

PERSISTENCE

Another key to effective praying is persistence. Luke says Jesus taught his disciples to always pray and never give up (18:1). Have you prayed about something for several days and then said, "God is not going to do it; God is not hearing me; it is not going to work out"?

When you learned how to walk, you fell a few times, didn't you? When you were riding a bike, you didn't fall off that bike and say, "I will never learn to ride. I'm just quitting. I will just walk the rest of my life." You kept on until you finally got it. One key to prayer is persistence. If you and I are going to be men and women who are effective in prayer, we have to be committed to staying with it.

BE YOURSELF

A key idea that really may free us some in prayer is to be yourself. Have you heard a lofty-sounding, high-church prayer? "O Lordest, thouest Godest blessest us herest tonightest." If you talk that way, pray that way. The way you usually talk is the way you should pray. Talk to God as naturally as you do your family and friends. When you approach God, be yourself. Don't try to impress Him with your words. He loves you, but He is not impressed with your vocabulary. Be yourself when you talk to God. See, that is freeing, isn't it? We do not have to come to God and be religious. Just be yourself when you pray.

PRAYER IS ABOUT RELATIONSHIP

When you pray, remember, prayer is about relationship. I firmly believe the only person who has a true prayer life is a Christian. Doesn't it make sense that before Jesus wants to grant your petitions He wants to have your heart? Prayer is about relationship. It is about having a relationship with Christ, and your relationship to Jesus is paramount to how well your prayer life will thrive. If you are away from God, you need to get your heart right before you can have a good prayer life. Being in a right relationship with Jesus is very important.

SUBJECTS TO PRAY ABOUT

There are several subjects we need to include when we pray. Every time you pray you will not need to complete this list, but you need a time in your day you set aside to pray. And when you do, you need to consider these things because they are biblical aspects of prayer.

When the disciples asked Jesus to "Teach us to pray," the Bible word *pray* they used was an *all-encompassing* word. It could mean thanking God. It could mean praying for others or asking for something for yourself. Other words for prayer in the New Testament are used specifically for asking. Jesus was teaching us how to pray in this passage in Matthew, chapter six, but He does not mention here everything that can be encompassed in prayer. He does not talk about thanking God or praying in Jesus' Name, but He does lay out some fundamental guidelines.

PRAISING GOD

We need to bring to God various kinds of prayer when we pray. One great way to begin your prayer time is by praising God. Jesus said, "When you pray, say: 'Father, hallowed be your Name, holy and honored is your Name.' " Praising expresses the wonder and admiration we have for who He is.

Many verses in the Bible tell us to praise God. Psalm One Hundred says "Enter His gates with thanksgiving and His courts with praise." But as strange as this may sound, praise is a hard part of prayer for most people. That is because we are not naturally at ease praising other people. What is praising God? Praising someone else or praising God is telling them you love them and you think they are wonderful.

There is a difference between thanksgiving and praising. Thanksgiving is simple; I thank you for what you do. I praise you for who you are. This is a good illustration. Suppose my wife and I are invited to dinner and the hostess cooks a terrible meal. I would not be truthful if I said to her, "You are a wonderful cook," but I can honestly thank her for what she did. If she were a great cook, I could praise her as well as thank her for the food. I could praise her for being a wonderful cook.

When I go to God, I need to thank Him for what He does. I need to praise God for who He is. I need to pray saying, "Jesus, I love You. God, I love You. Holy Spirit, I love You." And I need to admit, "Lord, this is difficult and unnatural to me, so You help me learn to praise Your Name, God." We need to praise God when we pray.

FORGIVE OTHERS

A very important preparation for coming to God is to have our hearts right with other people. When Jesus prays, "God, forgive us our sins for we also forgive everyone who sins against us," He is talking about an act that has already taken place. Matthew 6:14-15 contain words written to Christians after the time He had given them the Lord's Prayer. Jesus said, "If you forgive men when they sin against you, your heavenly Father will also forgive you. But if you do not forgive men their sins, your Father will not forgive your sins." Here He is not talking about salvation; He is talking about relationship.

When Jesus said that as a Christian my heart toward you is going to affect my relationship toward Him, He meant what He said. He was very serious. And those words of Jesus Christ apply to us today every bit as much as they did to the disciples. An extremely important part of my prayer life is getting my heart right with other people. I cannot go to God and ask Him to help my family and my life if I am bitter toward you. That is powerful, but that is true.

CONFESS YOUR SINS

Another thing in prayer which follows right along with that is the confession of sin. Jesus says, "God, forgive us our sins." First John 1:9 was written for Christians, and it says that, as Christians, "If we confess our sins, he is faithful and just and will forgive us our sins...." It is not that we need to be forgiven again for salvation, but we do need to be forgiven for our fellowship with God to be restored.

Psalm 66:18 is a verse every Christian should learn. It says "If I had cherished sin in my heart, the Lord would not have listened ...

and heard my voice in prayer." What that means is if I am coming to God and there is sin in my life I am not dealing with, I need not expect God to grant me my wishes.

Prayer is about relationship, and if I am not right with you that hinders my prayer life. I need to get right with you in my heart. If I am not right with God, I need to do my best to get right with God. Confession of sin is a very important aspect of prayer.

THANKSGIVING

Thanking God is also vitally important to our prayer life. Remember, we praise people for who they are, and we thank them for what they do. God graciously does many things for us and gives us much for which we should express our gratitude to Him. First Thessalonians 5:18 is the classic verse, "Give thanks in all circumstances, for this is God's Will for you in Christ Jesus." We should spend time thanking God when we pray.

INTERCESSION

Our prayers need to include intercession. Intercession simply means I pray for other people; I go before God on behalf of others. Jesus says "Give *us* each day our daily bread." That is plural, and it implies praying for others. Many other passages in Scripture support that action. First Timothy 2:1 says, "I urge then, first of all, that requests, prayers, intercession and thanksgiving be made for everyone...." We need to pray for other people.

PRAY FOR YOURSELF

And this—we need to pray for ourselves. "God, give *us* our daily bread." I will pray for you to have your daily bread, but I want mine, too. "God, give *me*." I pray for myself. You need to pray for you. No one in the world knows your heart and your needs like you do. I hope you do not tell everybody everything that is on your heart. You probably do not; you are smart if you do not. You tell God. You need to pray for yourself.

LISTENING TO GOD

One last part of prayer that so often is left out is listening to God. Do you know when you pray, you ought to listen, too? God not only through Scripture but also through prayer wants to speak to us, and we need to listen to God. Charles Stanley wrote a great book called *How to Listen to God.*[3] Read that book and it will bless your life.

PRAY TO LEARN HOW TO PRAY

One thing I think is exciting about the disciples' request is they saw everything Jesus did. They watched as He healed people. They saw Him do some really impressive miracles. Yet, we have no record of them ever saying, "Jesus, teach us how to do a miracle," or "Jesus, teach me how to preach like You," or "Teach me how to teach so my Sunday School class will go 'wow.' " No, they said, "Jesus, teach us how to pray." Do you think perhaps they figured out that the power for everything else flowed from His prayer life? I believe that is true.

Jerry Rankin is the president of the International Mission Board of the Southern Baptist Convention. In 1994, he was talking about prayer, and he said something that for a man in his position was very humbling. He said at one point in his spiritual journey he realized his spiritual life was not what it should be. In fact, at best, it was mediocre. He knew he did not have the spiritual strength and power he once had.

As he studied what was wrong with his spiritual life, he realized the problem was his prayer life. Oh, he could argue the Bible. He knew the Hebrew and the Greek. He knew the theology. But he had let his prayer life grow weak.[4]

BECOME A PERSON OF PRAYER

How is your prayer life? Or how do you want your prayer life to be? Maybe you have never given your life to Jesus. What you need to do is to come to Christ. I hope you will give yourself to Him and be born again. Then become part of a praying church, a church that follows Christ.

Christian, the lack of power or the lack of fruit in your life may be because your prayer life is weak. Perhaps you read devotional books or the Bible, but you still hurt in your heart and you are not praying like you should. Come back to Christ in your prayer life. Say, "God, I want to learn how to pray. God, I want to learn to pray and to be a man or woman of prayer." I promise you, those are prayers that God will hear and respond to!

Do you want to have a strong prayer life?
Begin by giving your life to God.
Learn how at *www.fbcruston.org*

2

PRAISING GOD WHEN WE PRAY

Do you like to be told you are wonderful, you are great, you are fantastic, and that you are adored? We like that, don't we? We enjoy that; we enjoy being praised. We love having someone honor us. God enjoys that, too. I want us to look at an aspect of prayer that is greatly neglected but very important, and that is praising God when we pray.

PRAISE GOD

What does it mean to praise someone? The Old Testament gives us a great example:

> David praised the Lord in the presence of the whole assembly, saying, "Praise be to you, O Lord, God of our father Israel, from everlasting to everlasting...
>
> Now, our God we give you thanks, and praise your glorious name.
>
> 1 Chronicles 29:10, 13

The Hebrew Old Testament word praise is a very significant word. It means *to be bright* or *to shine* or *to honor, to celebrate, to glorify, to cause to shine* or *to radiate*. That is a beautiful word, isn't it? It means to honor or exalt someone.

There are differences in thanking someone and praising someone. We thank someone for what they have done. We praise someone for who they are. I thank you for what you do. I praise you for who you are. Thanksgiving focuses on the deed; praise focuses on the person.

Let's say someone comes to sing in church, and they don't sing very well. Their voice is not great, but they sing a solo and try really hard. You thank them, don't you? You thank them for trying. "Thank you for the message we received from your words." But if someone comes and does a beautiful job, not only can you thank them but you can praise them for their voice and their ability.

Thanksgiving focuses on the deed; praise focuses on the doer. To praise someone is to brag on them, to express your positive feelings. Praise is simply to express your love and admiration.

PRAISE GOD IN PRAYER

We need to make praising God a top priority in our prayer life.

FOCUS ON GOD BY PRAISING GOD

David praised the Lord. Was David leading worship? Maybe, but I believe he was praying at this point. His focus was on God, and he was praying. He was praising God in prayer.

Praising God needs to be a focus in our prayers. We need to lift up the Name of Jesus Christ. We need to lift up the Name of God. We need to honor God when we pray to Him.

Praising ought to be something you do at the beginning of your prayer time. You should pray throughout the day. I hope you do. I hope you pray when crises come up during the day. But I hope, too, you are setting aside a definite time for prayer each day.

When you pray, there are things you need to include besides just asking God to bless you and to give to you. Some of the things you need to include are getting your heart right with others and confessing your sins. And one thing you should do at the beginning of your prayer time is to devote time to praising Jesus Christ.

JESUS BEGAN PRAYER WITH PRAISE

Matthew shows us Jesus' priority in prayer. He shows us in the Lord's Prayer when Jesus was teaching His followers how to pray, the very first thing He told them was, "Say this: 'Our Father in heaven, hallowed be your name' " (6:9). Luke also said Jesus taught the disciples to talk to God this way: "Lord, hallowed be thy name" (11:2).

That word *hallowed* means God, *high and lifted up and honored* be your Name. In Jesus' world and in Jesus' culture, a name was more than just an identification tag. It was a reflection of your character, who you were. So Jesus said, "When you begin to pray, focus your attention on God and praise Him." Begin your prayer time by saying, "God, I want to start this time with You by saying You are wonderful, You are holy, You are great."

Jesus was teaching us how to develop our prayer time and how to structure it. We need to begin praying with our focus on Him, praising God and praising His holy Name.

PRAISE GOD THROUGHOUT THE DAY

Certainly, do not limit your praise of God just to your quiet time or your devotional prayer at the beginning of the day. Praise God all through the day. Praise God through the day anytime you think about Him.

When I was in seminary, I was in a class where we were talking about developing our spiritual lives, and the professor challenged us. He said, "I want you during this semester to try to praise God throughout the day every hour you are awake. How you remember to do that, whether it is when the big hand strikes the hour or you write yourself a note, every hour take even just thirty seconds and praise God." I want to tell you that is a great thing.

We cannot express praise for God enough; we cannot tell Him enough that we love Him; we cannot honor Him enough. I believe the Bible tells us praising God needs to be a priority of our prayer life. I believe it is something we ought to begin our prayer with, and I believe it is something we ought to try to do throughout the day.

HOW DO WE PRAISE GOD?

How do we praise God? This can be awkward. When I became a Christian, I understood the need to tell God I did something wrong. I understood I needed to thank Him and to ask Him for blessings for other people and for myself, but praising God was something that was not natural. It was not something I had been taught or that had been modeled for me.

EXPRESS YOUR PRAISE VERBALLY

How do you praise God? Verbally express your praise to Him. David did not say, "God, you know my heart." No, David praised the Lord. He said, "Praise be to you, O Lord, God of our father Israel, from everlasting to everlasting." David honored God in his heart, but it came out through His mouth. He expressed to God verbally his love for Him and his adoration for Him.

You have heard the story of the couple celebrating their fiftieth anniversary. They were riding around their farm admiring their cattle and their beautiful land. The wife looked at her farmer husband and said, "There is something that has been bothering me for about forty-nine and a half years."

He said, "Well, what is it?"

She answered, "The day we married you told me I was wonderful, and beautiful, and you loved me, but in the last fifty years you have not told me that again. Why is that?"

He looked at her and said, "Honey, I told you fifty years ago you were wonderful, and great, and I loved you, and that if I changed my mind I would let you know."

That makes a funny story, but it does not make a good marriage, does it? With God, it is the same. With people and with God, we need to put into words our good and loving feelings toward them.

How do you praise God? Express it. Put into words what is on your heart. Tell God you love Him. Tell the Holy Spirit you love

Him. Tell Jesus Christ the Son you love Him. Tell the Father, Son, and Holy Spirit they are wonderful and magnificent and great. This is something most of us are not in the habit of doing, so it is new. Tell God you love Him. Express verbally your feelings to God.

Sing Praise to God

A second way we can praise God is to sing to Him. Some of us may need to make sure other people are not within hearing distance. Find an old hymn or a new praise chorus and sing that to God. You might sing "How Great Thou Art" or something totally different. God loves those beautiful old hymns, and He loves a beautiful new chorus. He loves anything that touches people's hearts and glorifies Him. Praise Him through music. Sing praises to God.

Read Scripture to God

Another way you can praise God is to select a psalm from the Old Testament, Psalm 148, 150, or many others. Open your Bible and say, "God, I want to express this to you. I want to read this to you." Many of those psalms were written as prayers or songs. Pray them to God.

With our old sinful, broken nature this is not easy and natural. We are selfish and prideful. Therefore, praising God does not come naturally. When you begin to do this, you may think this is just not comfortable; it does not feel natural. That is okay. Keep doing it. Praise God through song or by reading Scripture to Him. Or simply from your heart say, "God, I just want to tell You, I love You." "Jesus, I praise You. You amaze me." "Holy Spirit, You are wonderful." Doing that is praising God.

REASONS TO PRAISE GOD

Praise heightens the awesome sense of privilege we have being in God's presence. Here are some very important reasons we should praise God every time we approach Him in prayer.

Jesus Told Us to Praise God

One reason to praise God is we are told to do this. In Matthew 6:9, when Jesus was teaching us how to pray, He said begin your prayer time saying, "God, holy and honored are You and Your Name." Praising God is obeying Jesus. If you want to please God, praise God.

God Deserves Our Praise

God deserves our praise. He is worthy of our love and adoration, and as we acknowledge who He is we need to express to Him our sense of His greatness. Here are a few reasons God deserves our praise.

God Is Creator of All

God is deserving of our praise because He is the Creator. Scripture tells us of His supremacy.

> Yours, O Lord, is the greatness and the power and the glory and the majesty and the splendor, for everything in heaven and earth is yours. Yours, O Lord, is the kingdom; You are exalted as head over all.
>
> 1 Chronicles 29:11

Genesis 1:1 says, "In the beginning God created the heavens and earth." One reason we ought to praise God is He created it all.

I heard a scientist say when you look up at the night sky the stars you can see are a miniscule part of what is there. He said if you have been to the ocean and have looked down and have seen some fish, you have not seen very many fish considering how many are in the ocean. And he said that is about how many stars you are seeing compared to what is in the sky.

Do you know the Bible says God put every star up there? God is the Creator of it all. God is worthy of our praise. The Milky Way Galaxy, which we and our sun are in, is said to include maybe a hundred billion stars. Some astronomers have said there may be a hundred billion other galaxies out there.

How big is a hundred billion? If you were to start tonight counting and count to one hundred billion, and you count to two hundred and fifty every minute, and you never slept and you never stopped counting; you would reach one hundred billion in a thousand years. That is a pretty big amount, isn't it?

And what is so special about that hundred billion stars or galaxies is that God created them all. That is awesome, isn't it? Yes, that is awesome. God is worthy of our praise.

God Is Ruler over All

God deserves our praise not only because He created everything but because He rules over it all. He controls it all.

> Wealth and honor come from you; *you are the ruler of all things.* In Your hands are strength and power to exalt and give strength to all.
>
> 1 Chronicles 29:12

Not only did God create it all, God rules it all. Several years ago it was popular to wear t-shirts that said, "Girls Rule," or "Boys Rule." Those were cute. The truth is God rules. God not only created it all; He rules it all. He is the Creator and King of it all.

There is a beautiful song, "Our God is an awesome God. / He reigns from heaven above / with wisdom, power and love. / Our God is an awesome God!"[1] God is worthy of our praise. He is the Creator of all, and He is the King of all.

God Is Loving

God deserves our praise because He is loving. "For God so loved the world ..." (John 3:16). Think about the uniqueness of this. The God who created everything and rules everything looks down from heaven and notices you and me.

Have you ever flown in an airplane? When you get to 30,000 feet, a house looks like it is not very big. I think flying in an airplane is humbling. It is to me. It makes me realize I am not as big as I thought I was. And God looks down and sees everything, but He still takes notice of you and me. God is worthy to be praised because He is such a loving Creator.

GOD LOVES OUR PRAISE

Let me give you another reason we ought to praise God. God loves our praise. God loves your praise. He loves my praise. "Now, our God, we give you thanks, and praise your glorious name" (1 Chr. 29:13). Scripture says that God inhabits the praises of His people (Ps. 22:3). He dwells where people praise Him. God loves our praise. Why should we praise God? We should praise God because He loves it. It honors Him. It pleases Him.

Scripture tells us God has emotion. God gets angry. God becomes broken-hearted. God is joyful, and I believe God can be happy. God is touched in a special way by our expressions of praise. Jesus Christ is the perfect picture of the Father. Jesus who walked on earth is the perfect picture of what is in heaven, and what He shows us is our praises bless God.

In another seminary class, we were discussing different churches and denominational groups and why some of them seemed to be growing and flourishing and others did not. This was in the late eighties when many new charismatic churches were really beginning to blossom and do well.

I will never forget what one professor said. He said, "I believe some of these charismatic churches are being blessed by God because they are praising God." Praising God is for everyone. When we praise God, we honor God. God loves that. Whether it is with the church body or individually, we please God when we praise God.

PRAISING GOD BLESSES US

Praising God blesses us. As you read these verses, "David praised the Lord in the presence of the whole assembly, saying, 'Praise be to you, O Lord, God of our father Israel, from everlasting to everlasting. You are the ruler of all things,'" do you believe David was grouchy or unhappy? I want to tell you he was energized at this point. When you and I begin to develop a lifestyle of praise, it changes us. It changes our focus when we praise God.

I remember two old country guys talking, and one of them was trying to tell about the difference a focus on God can bring to you. He said, "You know before I was a Christian, I saw a pig in the mud, and all I saw was the pig in the mud. Now I see a pig in the mud, and I also see bacon in the pan. God has changed my focus." What happens is God helps us see the pig and the bacon in the pan. It changes our focus when we praise God.

Dr. Joel Gregory is a great preacher. He pastored some great churches and has preached literally around the world. As a young minister working on his master's degree and pastoring a small church he became deeply depressed and felt like the people in his church did not like him.

One Sunday without telling his wife, without telling anybody, he resigned. He said it hurt the church and hurt him and his wife, but he did it. They packed their things and moved to Ft. Worth. He said his grades began to drop. He began selling encyclopedias door-to-door. The added stress increased the depression. He said he planned to quit school at the end of the semester.

But someone said to him, "Joel, I want to challenge you to begin to praise God." He may have gone to a doctor, too. I do not know about that, but I do know he began to praise God. And he said focusing on lifting up and praising God changed his life.

Now, I am not telling you praising God will bring you out of a clinical depression, but it can help you. It can make you feel better. It changes your outlook, and it changes your heart.

Dr. Gregory went back and told that church, "I made a mistake. I want to come back." The church voted again, and he received a better vote the second time. And he attributed much of his recovery to praising God.[2] Praising God blesses us.

DECIDE TO PRAISE GOD IN YOUR PRAYER LIFE

Why do we not praise God like we should? It blesses us. It pleases Jesus. It is something we should do. He is worthy of it. Why don't we do it? Why don't we praise others like we should? Most of us give praise reluctantly. Break that habit. Become a person who certainly praises others but who also develops a lifestyle and a prayer style of praising God.

If you are not a Christian, give your life to Christ. That will give you a great reason to praise God. If you are a Christian and you are away from God, come back to God. God loves you and is worthy not only of your praise but of your life.

Make praising God a fundamental part of your daily prayer time and your lifestyle. Not only is it a right thing to do, it is a life-changing thing to do. I challenge you to make that commitment.

Do you want God to enjoy your prayer life with you?
Welcome Him with pleasant words of praise.
Praising God is a big part of what we do at www.fbcruston.org

3

IF YOU WANT YOUR PRAYERS ANSWERED, YOU'D BETTER BE RIGHT ON THIS ISSUE

Several years ago, I read an autobiography of a great athlete. The story was very interesting, but some things I read disturbed me. One thing that disturbed me was how he struggles with an unforgiving spirit.

He told two stories from his life where this was manifested. One was when he was a young person, a youth growing up. Someone hurt him and did him wrong. He made the comment years later that if he ever ran into that person he was going to get them back. Clearly, he had not forgiven them.

He also told a story that happened during his professional career. One of his teammates made a comment that was not very nice or kind. Later, he came back and apologized, but the player said, "I'm not going forgive you. I don't do that. I'm not into this 'forgiving people.'"

You know, that is a strong statement, and I want us to look at why that is so wrong. It probably is a prevalent attitude, but it is a wrong attitude. As we continue our study of prayer, we will look at forgiving others as a major issue of prayer. We have considered praising God as a necessary part of our daily prayer life. Now we need to look at forgiving other people as a vital aspect of our daily prayer life.

DOES GOD HEAR OUR PRAYERS?

People want God to hear their prayers. I earnestly believe that. I have never heard a person say, "I don't care if God hears my prayers." Some people do not pray, and they admit they do not, but I have never heard anyone say, "I don't care if God hears my prayers."

We are told in the Bible there are times God does not or will not hear our prayers. Psalm 66:18 says, "If I had cherished sin in my heart, the Lord would not have listened." If I have unconfessed, unresolved sin in my life as a Christian, God is not going to respond to my prayers.

Dr. Roy Fish, an evangelism professor at Southwestern Seminary, was teaching a class I was attending on spiritual growth and development, and Dr. Fish explained this. He said it is not that God does not hear the prayer; it is that God will choose not to answer that prayer.[1] That really is alarming when you think about the crucial times of life when you may be facing an emergency or you may have a child in an ICU unit; you want God to hear your prayers. It is very important for us to understand God does not always respond to our prayers and that prayers are not answered on the basis of our beliefs or our philosophies.

PRAYER WORKS ON GOD'S TERMS

We must understand that prayer works on God's terms. There are many views on prayer and many sermons and books on prayer. Some of them are good. Some are not very good. Much of what is available is based on opinion that is not well-founded. When it comes to prayer, it is important to understand real prayer must be done on God's terms, not on our terms.

UNFORGIVEN SIN BLOCKS PRAYER

It is a basic principle of prayer that when as Christians our sins are not forgiven, our prayers will not be answered. Christians need to confess their sins, but here the emphasis is on being forgiven. When our sins are not forgiven, our prayers will not be answered. "Forgive us our debts, as we also have forgiven our debtors" (Matt. 6:12). Having our sins forgiven is of paramount importance for us to have a Christian prayer life.

Psalm 66:18 reminds us, "If I had cherished sin in my heart, the Lord would not have listened." When we have unconfessed sin in our life, sin we are not dealing with, our prayer life becomes blocked. Proverbs 28:13 says this: "He who conceals his sins does not prosper, but whoever confesses and renounces them finds mercy."

A very powerful passage of Scripture is Isaiah 59:1-2.

> Surely the arm of the Lord is not too short to save, nor His ear too dull to hear. But your iniquities have separated you from your God. Your sins have hidden His face from you, so that He will not hear.

This is not saying that as a Christian you will lose your salvation. It is saying Christians do sin. And when we do not deal properly with those sins, and we do not confess them, but deny them, ignore them, and continue to wallow in them; that hurts our fellowship with God. Unconfessed sin, or sin we have not dealt with in our lives, hinders our prayer life.

Forgive Others to be Forgiven

We must also understand when we are unforgiving toward others, our prayers will go unanswered. Jesus said, "This, then, is how you should pray ..." (Matt. 6:9). In the Sermon on the Mount, recorded in Matthew 5, 6, and 7, He was teaching what we now call the Lord's Prayer, though it probably would be more appropriate to call it the Disciples' Prayer.

Jesus was not teaching lost people how to be saved but saved people how to live. Matthew says when Jesus saw the crowd, He went up on a mountainside and sat down. His disciples came to Him, and He began teaching them (5:1-2). Jesus, in this sermon, was teaching Christians how to live and how to pray.

Jesus taught them to ask God to forgive them their debts, as they also had forgiven their debtors (Matt. 6:12). It is interesting that the only part of this prayer Jesus expounds further is this part about forgiving others. In the following verses, Jesus says, "For if you forgive men when they sin against you, your heavenly Father will also forgive you. But if you do not forgive men their sins, your Father will not forgive your sins" (14-15). Mark repeats this thought Jesus expressed that if we do not forgive others, He will not forgive us (11:25).

NOT FORGIVING OTHERS IS SIN

This leads us to understand that not forgiving others is sin. Very simply, it is. When I have bitterness, resentment, and an unforgiving spirit toward you or someone else, for me as a Christian that is sin. That is sin I must deal with for my prayer life to be free and powerful. And this specific sin causes Christians not to be forgiven. Jesus says, "For if you forgive men when they sin against you, God will forgive you." When you do not forgive others, your Father will not forgive you.

For me as a Christian to refuse to forgive others is sin. That in itself blocks my prayer life. What God says in such a powerful way is this sin of not forgiving others makes God unwilling to forgive me. I have to forgive you as a Christian before I can go to God and ask Him to forgive me, expecting Him to do that before I can have an open prayer life. This is extremely important. When I do not forgive, God does not forgive. And in both instances, my prayer life has been rendered ineffective.

In the 1700s, James Oglethorpe was a famous British general. General Oglethorpe, in talking with the great religious leader John Wesley, supposedly told him, "I never forgive. I don't forgive people who do me wrong."

Wesley looked back at him, and he said, "Then General, you'd better never sin."

There is great truth to that.

FORGIVING OTHERS IS VITAL TO OUR OWN WELL BEING

The English poet Lord Herbert said, "When we fail to forgive other people, we break the bridge we ourselves must cross." Forgiving other people is essential to having God forgive us as Christians, and our forgiveness is absolutely essential to our having God's ear when we pray.

I read an article by a therapist who said that when it comes to forgiving others, it is vital to our physical health. It is vital to our emotional health. We have to forgive other people.

I would add something else to what he said. Forgiving others is vital to our prayer life. If praying and connecting with God when you pray is important to you, please, understand that forgiving others is not an option; it is an absolutely essential part of it.

FORGIVE OTHERS TO BE RIGHT WITH GOD

Forgiving others must be part of the way we live and part of the way we pray. The great New Testament scholar Dr. William Barclay said, as he looked at this passage in Matthew 6: 14-15, it is frightening to think that as a Christian when I do not forgive others, my unforgiveness towards them blocks God's forgiveness in my own life.[2]

It blocks my own prayer life. This is frightening. It is crucial we be right on this for our own effectiveness, our own happiness, and our own prayer life.

WHAT FORGIVENESS MEANS

Forgiving someone does not mean you approve of their sins. We can hate what people do, disapprove strongly of what they do, but still care about *them*. Forgiveness never means you have to approve of the wrong they have done to you or to anyone else. Forgiveness does not even mean you have to be involved with that person anymore. Let me give you a few instances.

Suppose you have an employee working for you and as his supervisor you discover he is dishonest. He may steal from your company or cause trouble. You may even have warned him and written him up, but the problem continues. You can fire that person, and probably you would be unwise to hire him back without evidence of a true change of heart and a real difference in his life. But you must forgive him. Forgiveness does not mean you have to keep him on or rehire him. It means in your heart you have to let it go.

Perhaps you are dating. Let's say you are in a dating relationship with someone who wrongs you repeatedly. God certainly may tell you that you should breakup with that person. Your own intelligence should tell you that you should breakup with him, and move on, and not date him again unless you know of some great change that happens in his heart and life.

Forgiveness does not require you to continue to date that individual or be around him. It may work out where you can, but forgiving him does not mean you must continue to be involved with his life. It simply means you have to let go of that very emotional issue.

"For, if you forgive men when they sin against you, your heavenly Father will forgive you" (Matt. 6:14). That Bible-word *forgive* means *to leave something* or to *send it away*. That means you can hate what they have done. It may mean you do not want to be with them or be involved with them. Now, if they live with you in the same house or in the same dorm room, if they are part of your family or extended family, you may have to work through some of those things.

But what forgiveness means is you choose to move forward, you won't strike back, and you won't wallow around with hate in your heart and in your thoughts. It means to their face you are kind. It means behind their back you are kind. It means in your heart you will seek to have loving and kind thoughts and feelings toward them. That is easy to say, but how do you make it happen?

HOW SHOULD WE FORGIVE?

Forgiving others is a difficult struggle for most of us. A passage in the Lord's Prayer says, "Give us today our daily bread" (Matt. 6:11). One thing Jesus was teaching in this passage was the necessity of *daily* being in prayer and *daily* depending on God. Not only do we depend on Him for our physical needs like bread and the basic necessities of life, but we need to depend on God to help us forgive others.

FORGIVE REGULARLY

Forgiving others should be a daily part of your prayer life, something you do regularly. There may be something you have to work through regularly in your life with people. Don't fret about that. That's normal. It would be great if we could forgive people one time and it would be over and done, but sometimes that is not how it happens. Forgiving others is to be a constant pattern in our life.

PRAY FOR GOD'S HELP TO FORGIVE

Ask God to help you forgive people. Daily ask for that. Corrie ten Boom became a famous Christian author and speaker. Her personal story is sad but very interesting. She grew up in Europe in the wrong time of the twentieth century, and she and her sister were imprisoned in a Nazi concentration camp. During that time, they faced terrible hardships and suffering. They endured torture and many horrors. One particular German guard molested her and her sister and was very mean and brutal to them.

Years later, Corrie ten Boom was speaking about forgiving others and about the love of God. After the service a man came to speak to her. He did not recognize her, but she immediately recognized him as that particular German guard who had molested her and her sister.

He said to her, "Miss ten Boom, it is so great to hear your words about the love of God and about forgiveness because I have found that in my life, too."

She said her immediate reaction was not to thank him for his kind words but to have thoughts of hatred. She said immediately, right where they were standing, she asked God to forgive this man through her and to help her love him, and she said God did that for her.[3]

That may be a prayer you and I need to pray about certain people, and we may have to do it every day for a long time. Ask God to help you forgive people.

PRAY FOR THE OTHER PERSON

Another thing that will help you learn to forgive others is to ask God to bless their lives. Matthew said Jesus told His followers, "Love your enemies and pray for those who persecute you ..." (5:44). That is a very hard thing to do. But one of the great biblical principles to help us forgive people is to pray for them. Ask God to bless those people and to help those people who have hurt you or sinned against you or let you down.

You may not be able to mean a word you are saying. Tell God that. Say, "God, I do not mean this. Help me to mean it." But pray for them. Pray for them until you do mean it.

DEVELOP A POSITIVE MENTAL PICTURE

Something else you can do to help you forgive others is to develop a good mental picture of that person. Often when we are full of resentment and bitterness and that person's face pops up in our mind, we immediately put it behind a bull's eye or try to picture them with horns on their head and a pitchfork in their hand. Work on developing a positive mental picture of that person.

Let me recommend that you do this in the very first part of your prayer time. Do this praying to forgive others daily when you are having your devotional quiet time. Spend time praising God, and then ask God to help you forgive those you need to forgive.

"Forgive us our debts, as we also have forgiven our debtors" (Matt. 6:12). The verb tense is saying this: "God, we have already forgiven those people who have hurt us; now we ask You to forgive us." The Bible tells us this is the right order. Spend time praising God, and then spend time getting your heart right with other people. Do this at the beginning of your prayer time and certainly continue to do it throughout the day.

FORGIVE EVERYONE

Forgiveness is for everybody in your world and in your life. Years ago, Commius, who was the Duke of Florence, reportedly said the Bible says we must forgive our enemies, but it does not say we have to forgive our friends. I think he meant that as a joke or I hope he did. God says we have to forgive everyone.

Forgive Those Who Ask for Forgiveness

When someone comes to you and asks you to forgive them, you have to do it. You must forgive them.

Forgive Those Who Do Not Ask for Forgiveness

We are to forgive others when they do not ask. You and I know it can be hard to forgive someone when they ask. It can be even harder to forgive someone when they do not ask or when they do not even realize they should ask us for forgiveness.

God tells us to forgive those who sin against us not just when they ask but even when they do not ask. That will cover most of the hurts and pains you have with other people. Forgive them even when they do not ask.

Forgive People Who Hurt You Personally

Forgive people when they specifically hurt *you*. Jesus said, "For if you forgive men when they sin against *you* ..." (Matt. 6:14). When people hurt you personally or do you wrong or let you down, forgive them.

Forgive People Whose Sin Is Not Personal Towards You

Forgive people when they do something in general that is bad or wrong. The Bible wording says when they *sin*. Sometimes we are angry with people for things they have done, and they do not even know us. We may never even have seen them face to face, or we may have seen them only on television. We may be mad at Bill Clinton or George Bush.

Forgive people when they sin against the world or against your family member or your friend or when they do something wrong in the community. Forgive those who do things that are more general in your life.

Forgiveness is Crucial and Vital

Forgiving others is not optional. God didn't say for us to forgive people when they ask or when they are sorry. He said, "Forgive them." He did not say to forgive them when you feel like it or when you want to. He said, "Forgive them." It is an absolutely crucial thing for your prayer life.

You know the name Leonardo da Vinci. Leonardo da Vinci has many great stories, and he has an unforgiving story that is worth telling.

Leonardo da Vinci was the great intellect, the great thinker and painter. He is known for many of his great works. One, of course, is that beautiful painting, *Last Supper.*

The story is told that as he was painting this picture, he became angry with one of his friends. They had a bitter disagreement that was not resolved. As Leonardo was painting the Lord's Supper, he painted the face of his enemy-friend on the picture of Judas. He painted Judas as the man with whom he was angry. And when people would come by and see the unfinished picture, they immediately would know who it was. They would say, "Look, he's Judas."

I am sure Da Vinci thought he was getting back at the man, but what happened in his own life is what will happen in yours. He got stymied. The story says when he was ready to try to paint the picture of Jesus Christ, he could not do it. He had no spiritual power, no spiritual creativity.

As he examined himself, he realized why. It was because of what he had done to his ex-friend with the picture of Judas. So he went back and painted out his enemy's face on Judas, repainted Judas, and went on to paint the beautiful picture of Jesus we have today, the beautiful picture of the Lord's last supper.

UNFORGIVENESS BLOCKS RELATIONSHIPS

Unforgiveness blocks relationships. I want to tell you that is exactly what an unforgiving spirit does. It blocks our relationship with other people; it blocks our relationship with God, and it renders our prayer life ineffective.

FORGIVE OTHERS AS YOU PRAY

I want to ask you where you are in your relationship with God. Where are you in your attempt to be a person of real prayer? Determine to become a person who prays as Jesus taught. If there is sin in your life or an unforgiving spirit, make it right. Take this seriously, and ask God to help you forgive others. Ask God to help you get rid of bitterness and resentment in your life, and do this daily as a part of your prayer life.

Is forgiving hard for you? Would you like help to pray? Register a prayer request at prayer@*www.fbcruston.org*

4

IF YOU WANT YOUR PRAYERS TO BE HEARD BY GOD, YOU'D BETTER BE RIGHT ON THIS ISSUE, ROUND TWO!

If I were to ask you what you prefer, would you prefer things to be hard or easy? Why is it we enjoy eating dessert, watching TV, having recess at school, taking a nap? Those things are easy, aren't they? They are enjoyable, and they are easy.

Some things in life are hard. They are important, but they are hard—dieting, exercising, studying. Those are hard things. But the hard things are very important, aren't they?

I want us to look at some verses out of First John, chapter one. They are about something hard, and that is confessing our sins. I want us to look at the confession of our sins as a key to prayer and as a part of prayer. This is a hard thing, but if you do not get this right, and a lot of people do not, you will falter spiritually in your growth, in your joy, and certainly in your prayer life.

CHRISTIANS STILL SIN

Christians still sin, and we need to confess our sins to receive God's forgiveness. There are people who do not believe this. Some of us recently were discussing the confession of sin, and a speaker to college students was mentioned who had said Christians do not need to confess their sins because they do not have to be forgiven. As the speaker answered the students' questions, he acknowledged that Jesus said in the Lord's Prayer we are to seek forgiveness of our sins, as we forgive others (Matt. 6:12). But he went on to say, "That was before Jesus died on the cross, and after He died on the cross nothing that happened before the cross applies to us." Biblically, that is a very dangerous position to teach or to hold.

MESSAGE TO CHRISTIANS

The following Scripture passage was written to First Century Christians.

> This is the message we have heard from him and declare to you: God is light; in him there is no darkness at all. If we claim to have fellowship with him yet walk in the darkness, we lie and do not live by the truth. But if we walk in the light, as he is in the light, we have fellowship with one another, and the blood of Jesus, his Son, purifies us from every sin.
>
> If we claim to be without sin, we deceive ourselves and the truth is not in us. If we confess our sins, he is faithful and just and will forgive us our sins and purify us from all unrighteousness. If we claim we have not sinned, we make him out to be a liar and his word has no place in our lives.
>
> My dear children, I write this to you so that you will not sin. But if anybody does sin, we have one who speaks to the Father in our defense—Jesus Christ, the Righteous One.
>
> 1 John 1:5-10, 2:1

God inspired John to write these words. The first recipients probably were gentile or non-Jewish churches that had sprung up, but God also intended this letter for you and me today.

A question arises at the beginning of this passage. To whom is he talking, to lost people or to saved people? I looked at the writings of Bible scholars in twenty-four commentaries. Twenty-two of the twenty-four scholars, who represent some of the best Bible scholars in the world, addressed the question: "To whom was John writing?" They concluded this was written by God through John to Christians. The best scholarship in the world affirms it, and I agree with these scholars that this is a passage written to Christians.

DENYING OUR SIN DECEIVES US

We still sin, don't we? You do sin. I sin. First John was written about sixty years after Jesus had gone back to heaven. It was written by John, the apostle who wrote the gospel of John. He was by then an old Christian leader. The church had been in existence sixty to seventy years, and some serious errors were being included in the teaching.

One of the errors was a teaching from a group called the Gnostics. They believed the body and the soul were separate and that the body was sinful and the soul was not sinful. So they taught whatever you did with the body really did not matter because it did not affect the soul. They believed sin really had no effect, and that, in fact, people could say, "We do not sin."

Isn't it interesting that John says, "If we claim to be without sin, we deceive *ourselves* and the truth is not in us? If we claim we have not sinned, we make God out to be a liar and his word has no place in us" (1 John 5:8, 10).

Remember, the New Testament was written in the Greek language. When verse eight tells us that when we claim to be without sin, it is talking about our sinful nature. It is saying, "Christian, if you think you do not still have a sinful nature, you are deceived. You are not deceiving your husband or your wife or your roommate or your friends. You are deceiving yourself."

When John says that if we claim we have not sinned, he is conveying the idea of committing acts of sin. A sinful nature does sinful things.

Paul discusses this in a lengthy passage in Romans. He says "I do things I do not want to do. The things I want to do, I do not do. The things I do not want to do, I do. What is wrong with me?" And he ends it saying, "By the grace of God, I will have victory; I will have the ultimate victory." Paul was saying, "I am still a sinner; I am still struggling with sin" (7:15-17, 24-25, *Author's paraphrase*).

I love the story about the teacher of a second-grade class in Sunday School who asked the children, "What must we do to be forgiven?" Now, you know what she was expecting or hoping for. One little boy raised a hand, and she said, "Johnny, what is the answer?" The little boy said, "We have to sin first." Yes, the little fella was right. And sin we do!

We make God out to be a liar if we say we do not have a sinful nature and we do not sin. That is just how wrong and foolish it is to claim we do not sin. We are only fooling ourselves because everybody else knows we still sin and we still do wrong.

CHRISTIANS STILL NEED FORGIVENESS

If you are a Christian and I am a Christian and we still sin, we still need forgiveness and cleansing, don't we? We do. First John 1:9 says, "If we confess, He forgives." *If* is a conjunction, and in this sentence it is introducing a condition. It is saying that forgiveness is conditional on confession. When as Christians you and I sin, it is offensive to God. It is wrong. Sin is sin, and God hates it. We need forgiveness and cleansing not to be saved again but to restore our fellowship with Jesus Christ.

John tells Christians to confess their sins to receive God's forgiveness. And again, when he says, "I write this so that you will not sin, but if you do, you have One named Jesus Christ who will stand in for you," John is talking to Christian people (1 John 2:1, *Author's paraphrase*).

CHRISTIANS HAVE ETERNAL SECURITY

John is not saying that as a Christian you need constantly to confess your sins and be saved again. You were saved when you became a Christian. God justified you before Himself. That means He made you right with Him *eternally*.

I hold that great belief of eternal security. I believe the Bible teaches that when we were saved we were justified before God. We will never again be condemned before God. We stand in a right position and relationship with God, and confession of sin is about maintaining and keeping that joy in your fellowship with God.

If you are a parent, you understand this. If you are a child, you understand this. If you have a child or parent, you have a relationship, a biological relationship. Nothing can end that relationship except death. Your child will always be your child. You will always be your parents' child. True, the fellowship may be strained. There are times you may not talk to your kids very much or your parents may not talk to you, but that does not invalidate the relationship.

The confession of sin is not for you to regain your salvation. You never lost it. Confession of sin is to keep a healthy, good and loving fellowship with Jesus Christ.

CHRISTIANS HAVE TRUE FELLOWSHIP IN CHRIST

Fellowship in a relationship depends on honesty and openness. Denial and deception are destructive to the trust needed for a positive relationship.

Dr. Zane Hodges is a New Testament professor who explains this so well. Dr. Hodges says:

> In modern times, some have occasionally denied that a Christian needs to confess his sins and ask forgiveness. It is claimed that a believer already has forgiveness in Christ (Eph. 1:7). But this point of view confuses the perfect position which a Christian has in God's Son (by which he is even "seated . . . with Him in the heavenly realms" [Eph. 2:6]) with his needs as a failing individual on earth.
>
> What is considered in 1 John 1:9 may be described as familial forgiveness. It is perfectly understandable how a son may need to ask his father to forgive him for his faults while at the same time his position within the family is not in jeopardy.
>
> A Christian who never asks his heavenly Father for forgiveness for his sins can hardly have much sensitivity to the ways in which he grieves his Father. Furthermore, the Lord Jesus Himself taught His followers to seek forgiveness of their sins....[1]

For one to say confession should not be a part of the Christian life is to misunderstand completely what First John, chapter one says. First John, chapter one is not about entering the kingdom; it is about maintaining good fellowship with God in the kingdom.

SINLESS PERFECTION IS A FLAWED TEACHING

The speaker who taught that confession of sin was not necessary was teaching a view called *sinless perfection*. That position holds that a Christian can advance in knowledge or become spiritual enough that he no longer sins. We know that is an untrue teaching because God says we all still sin. We all do have a sinful nature, and we all still sin.

In fact, 1 John 1:9 is written to tell Christians we sin and we need to confess our sins to receive forgiveness. It says that clearly. Matthew 6:12 says in the Disciples' Prayer that Jesus prayed, "Forgive us, God, our faults as we forgive others" (*Author's paraphrase*). Luke 11:4 describes a different context where Jesus says the same thing. There again, He tells us to ask for forgiveness.

The Great Commission, Jesus' last instruction and promise before He went back to heaven, tells us Jesus charged his followers to go and make disciples and teach them to obey everything He had commanded. Now, let me remind you, most of what Jesus commanded was given before the cross. Jesus expects us to obey what He taught, and those teachings did not change after the Resurrection.

Jesus' words before the cross apply to us as much as those He spoke after the Resurrection. When the Bible says a Christian needs to seek God for forgiveness, it is not to be re-saved but to maintain our fellowship with Him and to keep our prayer life flowing in intimate communion with Jesus.

CONFESSION OF SIN IS A KEY TO PRAYER

Confession of sin is a key to our prayer life. First John 1:9 also tells us that to not confess our sins means they will not be forgiven. If we confess, He forgives. The opposite of that is if we do not confess, we will not be forgiven.

Unconfessed Sin Hurts Your Prayer Life

God meant for us to understand confession of sin is important to our Christian life and especially important to our prayer life. The Bible teaches that if we do not deal with our sins effectively, it has a negative effect on our prayer life. It says if we confess, He forgives; if we do not confess, He does not forgive. As a Christian, not dealing with the sin in my life will have a terrible effect on my prayer life.

Psalm 66:18 says, "If I had cherished sin in my heart, the Lord would not have listened." Proverbs 28:13 tells us when we try to conceal our sins, it causes us problems. Isaiah 59:1-2 are powerful verses that ask if God's arm is too short to help or if His ear is too dull to hear. The answer is no, absolutely no. It is our sins that are negatively affecting our ability to connect with God.

I take God seriously here. And what I see from Scripture is this: when I do not deal with the sin in my life, when I do not confess my sin and deal with it as a part of my prayer life, I am going to have an ineffective and futile prayer life.

Confession Acknowledges Sin

That word *confess* in your Bible is a great word. It is a combination of two separate Greek words. One word meant *same* or *alike*. The second word meant *to say*. And what that word *confess* means when you put the two words together is *to say the same thing*. Confession of sin is saying the same thing about your sin that God says about your sin. What I say about my sin when I confess my sin is the same thing about it God says.

That means when I look at my actions and my behavior and my thoughts that are wrong, I do not say, "Oh, that is an accident," "Oh, that was a mistake," or "Oh, that was a boo-boo." I say, "This was sin." God calls that behavior *sin*. God does not say it is an accident. He calls it sin. When I confess my sins, I say the same thing about my sin God does. I confess: "It is sin."

Confession Accepts Responsibly

I also say, "It is my fault." This is tough, isn't it? It is easier to say it is another's fault. "God, this is sin I did, but it's his fault." God does not accept that. "Oh, God, it's my genetics. God, it's heredity. God, it's society that's made me this way."

No, to confess my sins means I not only say it is sin like God does but I must admit it is my fault. I must take responsibility for it and be specific in doing this. I must say, "God, I have been dishonest. God, I have thought things I should not have thought. I have said things I should not have said. I have lost my temper. I have been impatient, and it is my fault, God."

And I must say that with a desire to turn from it. That does not mean I will ever master it here on this earth, but I must have a true desire and a real intent to turn from that sinful behavior.

Confession of Sin Brings Forgiveness

The truly good news is when we confess our sins some really great things happen. God promises, "If we confess our sins, he is faithful and just and will forgive us our sins and purify us from all unrighteousness" (I John 1:9). God forgives us when we confess our sins and acknowledge our guilt. He is faithful and just to forgive.

That word *forgive* means *to send something away* or *to dismiss it.* Do you owe the bank any money, a car note or house note? Wouldn't it be neat to go to the bank tomorrow to pay on your house note and walk in and hear them say, "We dismissed it; we just sent away your note"? Or maybe you have pay a fine for a parking ticket or speeding ticket, and you go to court and the judge says, "I dismissed the case." That is what forgiveness is. It is God saying, "When you deal openly and honestly with your sin, I am going to dismiss it. I am going to wipe the slate clean." Isn't that beautiful?

Confession of Sin Brings Cleansing

And it does not end there. God says, "I want to cleanse you, to purify you." As a Christian, I am going to tell you from my own life I know I sin, and when I do not deal with my sin I feel yucky. I feel the guilt and the burden of it. But when I confess my sin, God cleanses me. He purifies me.

The Roman world in which John lived majored on cleanliness. For them to hear God could cleanse them spiritually, morally, and ethically was a beautiful thought. Isn't it neat to know when we confess our sins God doesn't laugh at us? He doesn't get mad at us. He cleanses us, and He forgives us. That is beautiful, isn't it?

I heard a story of a man who was struggling with sin in his life. He was a Christian, but he was not confessing his sin or dealing with it. He just wanted to get rid of the burden, so he began to write huge checks to his church every Sunday. His pastor realized what was happening and wrote him a letter that said, "Dear Sir, Thank you for your great contributions. If this unconfessed sin continues to gnaw away at you, feel free to continue to give generously like you have been."

I want to encourage you to give generously, but don't do it because you are trying to do penance. Confess your sins, and let God forgive you and cleanse you. That is freedom in Christ. Isn't that beautiful? That is wonderful.

Not only will you be forgiven and cleansed but the prayer doors will open. Psalm 66:18 is an ugly verse that says, "If I regard sin in my heart, God will not hear me." But First John, chapter one comes in and says, "Oh, but when I confess my sin and deal with it openly and honestly, God forgives me and He opens His ear to hear my prayers" (*Author's paraphrase*). Isn't that beautiful? Isn't that wonderful? That's what I want. That's what I need.

CONFESS YOUR SINS DAILY

Confession of sin must be a regular priority of prayer because it is a key to God's ear. Having a clean heart is a key to God's ear. I want that. And we need to pray this part of our prayer at the beginning of our quiet time.

First John 1:9 says, "If we confess our sins." The idea is that of a continuous action. You do not just confess your sins once and that end the sin in your life forever. Forgiveness requires regular attention to the work of confession. It needs to be repeated again and again.

Set aside a regular time to pray each day, whether in the morning or in the evening, and begin your prayer by praising God. Make sure your heart is right with others and confess your sins to God. Do this not only at the beginning of your prayer time but throughout the day when God brings to your mind things you do that you know you shouldn't.

I have heard the great evangelist Billy Graham say in more than one sermon to keep short accounts with God. When you blow it and do something wrong, deal with it then. It is harder to deal with after days of build-up. Whether it is garbage or sin, it just takes longer and gets worse if you delay. Keep short accounts with God. Do this daily, and do it continually throughout the day.

PRAY FOR GOD TO SHOW YOU YOUR SIN

Now, if you are asking, "How do I do this?" let me tell you. Here is a good starting point. When you are on your knees, just say, "God, show me the sin in my life," and put on your seat belt.

When I began to do that in college, I had some great arguments with God. I would say, "God, that's not sin."

And He would ask, "Who is God here?"

"God, You are, but You are mistaken on that. That motive was not sinful. That behavior was not sinful."

Then after we would wrestle a bit, God normally would win if I would do right.

Ask God to show you your sin. Now let me give you this preface. You might want to say, "God, show me as I can handle it," because God is perfect and holy, and when He begins to reveal truth in our hearts sometimes it is ugly for awhile. Ask God to show you your sins if you are struggling with this.

BE HONEST AND SPECIFIC IN CONFESSING YOUR SINS

When you confess your sins, be specific and open and honest with God. Notice that John said, *we*. John did not say if *you*, he said if *we*, including himself, confess *our* sins (1 John 1:9). The thought here is of being specific, of naming the sins, calling them by name.

I heard of a funny story that happened during a revival. It was a great revival at the church, and several counselors were at the altar. A man came down and began to talk to them. The counselors realized the man really was a Christian; he had just messed things up with sin in his life.

One of the counselors said to him, "You need to get on your knees and confess your sins and get right with God."

The man said, "Will you come with me?"

The counselor agreed. They knelt down, and the man began to pray, "Oh, God, if we have sinned, forgive us."

The counselor stopped him and said, "Don't say *if*. You *have* sinned. And don't say *we*. Don't include me in your mess."

You need to be honest with God. You need to pour out your heart to God. If you have lied, if you have stolen, if you have committed adultery, if you have been lustful, if you have been involved in things you should not have been; name those sins. Be honest and open and be specific with God.

I was talking with a man I believe was a Christian, but he was having a lot of problems. He did not have much power or joy in his life. He was not very effective with other people or with God, and for years he had a really hard time going to sleep every night.

As I talked with him, I found out he never spent any time confessing his sins. In fact, he believed he did not have to, that everything was fine.

I told him, "That is wrong. You need to confess your sins to God daily. And since you have not done this in years, it may be painful and long at first. But once you are in the habit of doing this daily and throughout the day, it will become a natural and good part of your prayer life."

He came back a couple of days later and said, "I can't do that. It is too hard. It makes me feel bad, and it hurts my self-esteem to do that."

You know, what this person had bought into was some phony psychology and some phony theology that looked in the mirror and said, "I'm good, I'm good, I'm good," as if saying, "I'm good," three times and turning around in a circle would make everything fine.

CONFESSION OF SIN BRINGS GOD'S RESPONSE

Sometimes you have to be broken before you can get better. The most positive thing you can do for yourself is to be honest with God about your sin. He will not laugh at you or make fun of you. He knows we are guilty. He has great compassion, and He is just waiting to forgive us. He is just waiting to cleanse us. Be specific and open and honest.

When we do this, we open the gates of heaven. Confession of sin has to be a key to our praying. It is a key to our prayer life. It is fundamental to prayer, and it needs to be part of our daily quiet time.

I once heard Dr. John MacArthur, a pastor and author from California, say the reason many Christians lack joy and power in their lives is because they are not consistently confessing their sins to God. Some have probably gone days, weeks, and maybe years without really coming clean to their Lord. He went on to say unless we regularly confess to God, we will never have the life or the prayer life we desire to have.

CONFESS YOUR SIN

Maybe you are a Christian but you need to spend some time pouring your heart out to God, cleaning things up.

As a Christian, your commitment may need to be to decide part of your prayer time is going to be dealing specifically and openly and honestly with your sin. Pray, "God, make me a man or woman of prayer with everything that means, including being honest about what is going on in my life." To do this will bring you true joy as well as give you freedom and power with God in prayer.

Is a burdened heart keeping you from praying?
Confess your sins to Jesus.
Learn more about Him at *www.fbcruston.org*

5

AN IMPORTANT PART OF PRAYER: THANKING GOD

I read a great but sad story a pastor in Illinois had happen not long ago. A couple came to his office asking for help. They said they were hungry and had not eaten in a few days. He knew he wanted to help them so he took them across the street to a convenience store. He bought them a sandwich, some chips and a drink, and he took them outside. They grabbed the food and drinks, and without even saying, "Thank you," they sat down and began to devour the food. They were noticeably hungry. The minister was satisfied he had helped them. The man took a big drink of his soda and then put it down. He made an ugly face and looked at the pastor and asked, "Is that diet?"

The minister said, "I could not help it. I just laughed out loud. I had people coming to me wanting something. They did not say please or thank you. They just wanted the help. I gave them the help, but they were ungrateful because it was a diet drink instead of the real thing." He said he laughed and he also wanted to cry because he knew that is how he often was toward God.

THANKING GOD

I want to lead you to think about thanking God as a regular part of your daily prayer life and to show you the need for intentionally setting aside time to thank God.

Psalm 118:1 says: "Give thanks to the Lord, for he is good; his love endures forever." What do we mean by "giving thanks?"

GIVING THANKS RECOGNIZES THE BLESSING

Thanksgiving includes two basic ideas. The first aspect of giving thanks involves recognition. The psalmist says, "Give thanks to the Lord for He is good." The Old Testament was written in Hebrew, and the Hebrew word *thanks* involves the idea of *recognizing* something, of realizing how you have been blessed or how you have benefited from something.

The first part of being thankful requires using your cognitive abilities. Instead of being like the man who was upset because he had a diet drink, you realize you have been blessed because someone has done something good for you.

GIVING THANKS EXPRESSES APPRECIATION

Thanksgiving involves recognition, and then it involves expression. "Give thanks to the Lord, for he is good." It is interesting that the Hebrew word for *thanksgiving* not only means *to recognize* but it also means *to declare* something. It literally means to throw something or to cast something out. It is a word used in other places in the Old Testament for admitting our sin. It means we recognize our sin and we declare it before God, and it is used in this context to talk about thanking God.

Thanksgiving begins when we recognize we have been blessed, and out of that awareness we declare and express our gratitude. If you give me a hundred dollars and I say thank you for that, two things have happened. I have recognized you have done something for me, and I have expressed that to you. That may sound simple, but we miss both of these parts sometimes. Sometimes we miss the first, which means we miss the second. Yet, sometimes we get the first;

we just do not do the second. To thank someone is to recognize you have been blessed and then to express appreciation for that.

Thanking God begins with recognizing what God has done for us and then expressing or declaring our appreciation for what He has done. Thanking God needs to be a fundamental part of our life. "Give thanks to the Lord, for He is good." Make thanksgiving a regular part of your life. Thank God throughout the day. Thank God as He blesses you. No matter what happens, there are things to be thankful for.

GIVE THANKS IN EVERYTHING

One interesting and often misunderstood verse of the Bible is First Thessalonians 5:18 which says, "Give thanks in everything, for this is the will of God for you in Christ Jesus." That does not say to give thanks *for* everything. Some things are demonic and evil and wrong, and you do not thank God for those things.

Matthew Henry was a great preacher in the 1700s. When he was an elderly gentleman, one afternoon he was robbed on his way home. That night in his journal he wrote some words that are timeless. He thanked God for his day and he said,

> God, I thank you that in all my years this is the first time I have been robbed. God, I thank you that they took my money and not my life. And God, I thank you that I was the one who was robbed and not the robber.

What a neat response. Matthew Henry did not say, "God, thank you that I got robbed and abused by a cruel person." But even in the midst of that awful experience, there was much for him to be thankful for.

GIVE THANKS REGULARLY

If you are interested in pleasing God, being thankful regularly as a habit of your life is something you should do. And do this not only as a regular pattern of life but set aside part of your daily prayer time to thank God. "Give thanks to the Lord, for he is good." I hope you have a time before you go to bed or when you get up in the morning you set aside to pray. If you do not already do this, I want to challenge you to begin.

We need to structure our prayer time so we do not just haphazardly send up wish lists to God. That is not how the Bible teaches us to pray.

We should not hurry through the time we set aside for prayer. Taking time to be alone with God and talk with Him is the way we express to God our gratitude. Taking time for prayer is a way we show God we love and value Him. We need to take time to praise God for who He is. We need to take time to get our hearts right with others. We need to take time to confess our sins. We need to take time to pray for others and for ourselves, and we need to take time to thank God.

Be specific about setting your time for prayer, and guard that time. Devote time during your prayer time to thanking God. Don't be careless about this and just try to fit it in when you can throughout the day. You have 1,440 minutes in a day, and you should reserve some of those minutes to pray. If you are serious about praying properly and praying in a way that pleases God, thanking God is something you need to include in your daily prayer time.

THANK GOD FOR ALL HE IS AND DOES

There are many things for which we should thank God. There is an endless list of things for which we should be grateful, and we should seek to communicate to God our appreciation by thanking Him.

THANK GOD FOR SALVATION

Thank God for His salvation. "Give thanks to the Lord, for he is good; his love endures forever" (Ps. 118:1). If you are saved, you have much to be thankful for. "Whoever believes in him is not condemned, but whoever does not believe stands condemned already …" (John 3:18). When you were lost, you had the hangman's noose around your neck. You were on your way to hell, and Jesus Christ saved you from that. You ought to be thankful for that. Here are some beautiful verses that talk about this.

[Give] thanks to the Father, who has qualified you to share in the inheritance of the saints in the kingdom of light. For he has rescued us from the dominion of darkness and brought us into the kingdom of the Son he loves....

Colossians 1:12-13

If you were in a house that was on fire, and somebody came in that house and rescued you from being burned alive or from dying from the smoke, would you thank them? I would spend the rest of my life thanking them. I want to tell you God is never going to weary of hearing you thank Him for saving your soul. We ought to thank God every single day of our lives we are not going to hell but we are on our way to heaven. We ought to thank God for His salvation.

THANK GOD FOR ANSWERED PRAYER

Another obvious thing we ought to thank God for is for answering our prayers. "Give thanks to the Lord, for he is good" (Ps. 118:1).

In Washington, D. C., several years ago a postal employee did an unofficial survey. He kept up with the number of letters written to Santa Claus asking for presents before Christmas. It was a ton of letters. He also paid attention to how many thank-you letters Santa Claus got after Christmas from the kids. Guess how many he got. He got one.

We may snicker and say, "Oh, those kids, they are just ungrateful. It is that younger generation. We would have been much better." No, we wouldn't. And you know that, and I know that.

The truth of the matter is we do the same thing to God, don't we? We spend months praying and begging God for something, and then we are casual in thanking Him for the answer to our prayer. For a prayer He may have answered years ago, God never tires of hearing you say, "Thank you, God, for answering that prayer."

Look at everything. Be sensitive to the details in your circumstances. When you ask God for something and someone comes and meets that need, acknowledge that God sent that person. "God, I

51

need money, help me." If somebody comes and gives you some money, be aware that God selected that person. Thank that person and thank God. Be great in begging God and asking Him to help you and bless you. He wants you to. But be just as great in thanking Him for His answer to your prayers.

THANK GOD FOR HIS PROVISIONS

We can thank God for things He just does for us even without our asking. I am amazed at the things I do not pray for that God just blesses me with. I am ashamed I have not prayed about them, honestly. Thank God not only for answered prayers but for all the other things He provides for you.

Thank God for the things you have. "Give thanks to the Lord, for he is good." Recognize what you have and thank God for it. If you have a car, be thankful. If you have a house, be thankful. If you have health, be thankful. There are plenty of people who have none of those things.

David Livingston was a great missionary. One day when he was older, he was sitting, holding his left knee, and crying. One of his friends saw him and said, "Brother David, what's wrong? Have you hurt your leg?" David Livingston answered with something that revealed a life committed to thanking God. He said, "No, I was just sitting here thinking I have walked many, many miles through my life. I have used this old left knee for every one of those miles, and I just stopped to thank God for this left knee He gave me." You might say, "That is foolish, that is childish." If you have to have your knee replaced, you may not think so. Thank God for what you have.

T.W. Hunt was a professor of music at Southwestern Seminary for years, and then he went to work for the Southern Baptist Convention as a prayer consultant. I remember hearing him talk about thanking God in prayer and about an experiment he did that may be worth your trying. He said he woke up one day and decided to thank God for everything he had. He said he woke up and put his feet on the floor, and he thanked God for the warm floor he had. He said he went into the bathroom, and he thanked God for the mirror, the warm water, and shower that he had. He said as he brushed his teeth, he thanked God for his teeth and for the toothbrush and toothpaste. He went on to say that it was overwhelming how much we have to thank God for.

You say, "Oh, that is silly." No, it is not. All those things are gifts from God. We could spend the rest of our lives thanking God for everything we have and never exhaust it. Thank God for what you have.

THANK GOD FOR HIS PROTECTION

Thank God for what he protects you from. "Give thanks to the Lord, for he is good." Do you ever thank God for things that do not happen in your life?

In January 1999, in my hometown of Jackson, Tennessee, two huge tornados hit on a Sunday evening not far from where my brother was living at the time. We waited a day or two, and then we got the good news they were okay. It didn't hurt him or anyone in his family, and it didn't hurt their property, but it destroyed places near them. You know what; we thanked God for what did not happen.

When you get home after a long trip, do you thank God your car didn't break down; you didn't have a wreck; you didn't get a ticket; you didn't injure yourself or anyone else? Do you thank God for the things He protects you from?

In 1990, Garth Brooks sang a song, "Thank God for Unanswered Prayers." Let me remind you what Garth said. He went to a high-school reunion, and he saw his old girlfriend that, apparently, he had prayed to God that someday he would marry. It had not worked out that way. Garth looked at his wife, and he said, "Thank God for unanswered prayers."[1]

There are prayers God has not answered for you and me that we should be thankful for. We should say, "God, thank You that you were smarter than I was and You did not listen to me in that instance." Thank God for what He has protected you from.

THANK GOD FOR WHAT HE IS GOING TO DO

Here is another thing we need to thank God for, and this is stepping out in faith. Thank God for what He is going to do for you. "Give thanks to the Lord, for he is good." Do you thank God for what He is going to do in your church, not just for what He has done but for what He is going to do? Do you thank God for what He is going to do in your life and in your family?

Be positive. Step out in faith. Thank God for what He is going to do. Before you attend church Sunday, pray that God will do something great. Thank Him for it. You do not have to ask Him, "God, if it is your Will, do something great at my church." It is His Will. Pray for it, believe it, and thank God for it. Thank God for what He is going to do.

THANK GOD FOR GOD

Thank God for God, and that is not redundant. Thank God for God. "Give thanks to the Lord, for he is good." We can praise God for who He is. "God, I praise You for who You are." Have you thanked God for what He does? When I am in the thanksgiving part of my prayer I like to say, "Jesus, thank You for leaving heaven and coming to earth. Thank You for dying on the cross. Thank You for walking out of that tomb. Thank You, Jesus, for what You have done for me."

"God, thank You that of all the ways You could have chosen to be, You chose to be loving and kind." He did not have to choose to be that way. When was the last time you said, "Holy Spirit, thank You that You live inside of me; thank You that You guide me, You convict me, and You comfort me"? You ought to thank God for God.

We ought to thank God for who He is, spending time expressing to the Father, Son, and Holy Spirit not only our praise but also our thanksgiving.

There is a Chinese proverb that says, "When you drink from the stream, remember the spring." When you are enjoying the water, remember the source. Thank God as a regular part of your life. Set aside time daily to thank Him.

THANKING GOD BRINGS POSITIVE RESULTS

Thanking God brings some positive results. Thanking Him does bring about some truly positive results.

THANKING GOD PLEASES GOD

Thanking God pleases God. "Give thanks to the Lord, for He is good." When you and I are thankful to God, we are being obedient. Do you want to be obedient to God? One way we express our obedience is by being thankful. First Thessalonians 5:18 reminds us to: "Give thanks in all circumstances, for this is God's will for you in Christ Jesus." As you and I thank God, we are doing His Will. We are being obedient by thanking Him.

Philippians 4:6 says, "Do not be anxious about anything, but in everything, by prayer and petition, with thanksgiving, present your requests to God." Anytime you obey God, you please Him because God is like you and me in that He appreciates our being thankful.

You are familiar with the story in Luke where Jesus healed ten people. Nine sprinted away. One of them came back and said, "Thank you." Jesus asked, "Where are the other nine?" Then He spent some time really blessing the one who came back (17:11-19).

Don't think of God as a cold, distant deity. God is very personal. The Bible says what we saw in Jesus is the same as the Father, and like you want to be thanked, God wants to be thanked. When we thank people and when we thank God, it blesses them.

THANKING GOD BLESSES YOU

Thanking God blesses you. "Give thanks to the Lord and praise his name." First of all, anytime you obey God, you are going to benefit from that. It may be hard at first. It may even be painful, but obeying God always blesses us.

THANKING GOD CHANGES YOUR FOCUS

Some very practical things happen when you thank God. One is it changes your focus.

Several years ago, a person I knew had her purse stolen. She was walking through a big-city parking lot, and a couple of teenagers ran up, grabbed the purse, and they got away.

She had lost some money and her billfold, and she had been scared, but as she began to reflect, she said, "I didn't get hurt, they couldn't use my credit cards, and it didn't cost me anything. I lost a little cash, but in the long run, I was okay." As she focused on how she had been blessed in that situation, it changed her attitude from negative to positive.

I want you to know if you thank God it will benefit you. You cannot spend two, three, five, or ten minutes regularly thanking God without it having an uplifting effect on you because it forces you to focus on good and positive things. It changes your focus.

THANKING GOD INCREASES YOUR FAITH

Another way thanking God blesses you is it increases your faith. How does that happen? It reminds you what God has done for you. It amazes me when I am facing problems and I spend time thanking God for how He solved similar problems five, ten, or fifteen years ago, I feel better because I am reminded God's bicep is plenty big enough for my problems. Thanking God increases my faith by reminding me who He is and what He can do.

A beautiful old song says, "Count your many blessings, / name them one by one, / and it will surprise you / what the Lord hath done."[2] It will amaze you, and it will increase your faith to remember what God has done because it helps you to believe He will do great things again.

God has not changed. God still *can* act and He still *will* act on your behalf. Thanking God reminds you of those great things in the past and increases your faith to believe what He can do today and what He will do in the future. Thanking God blesses God. Thanking God is obedience that pleases God and blesses you. Thanking God will change your focus. It will increase your faith, and it will remind you how great is the God you serve.

CHOOSE TO THANK GOD

An old fable is told of two angels that were carrying buckets to heaven, going to heaven and coming back down, going back up with buckets.

One day, someone caught them. He said, "I am going to let you go. I just want to know what is in those buckets."

One bucket was overflowing, and the angel said, "This is prayer requests from people asking things of God."

The man looked at the other bucket, and it was almost empty. He asked that angel, "What is this?"

The angel looked kind of sad, and he said, "These are thanksgivings going up to God."

I am afraid that is true, isn't it? I want to challenge you, let's fill both buckets.

God wants us to be thankful, and I want to encourage you to develop a lifestyle of prayer that includes a lot of thanksgiving to God. You and God both will be happy that you did!

Do you have a thankful heart?
Let it show. Tell others. Tell God.
We thank Him at <u>www.fbcruston.org</u>

6

THE POWER OF PRAYING FOR OTHER PEOPLE

We have had some terrible tragedies in our world in recent years. We all can think of people in our community and in our extended world who have great problems and are grieving. They may have financial problems, emotional or physical problems, or they may have spiritual problems. Maybe someone you care about is not a Christian. There is no greater problem in the world than not knowing Jesus Christ.

How is the best way to help people? How is the best way to help our missionaries? Certainly, money can help, but I don't think that is the greatest way. How do we help someone who is grieving? We want to help them even though we say we don't know what to do.

The greatest thing we can do for people is to pray for them. And as we consider our prayer time, we want to develop a prayer system for how to pray well for others.

We have looked at other parts of prayer: praising God, getting our hearts right with others, confessing our sins, and thanking God. Praying for other people is another extremely important part of prayer.

PRAY FOR OTHER PEOPLE

What does it mean to pray for others? The Old Testament gives us a great example from the life of Moses.

> The Lord said to Moses, "How long will these people treat me with contempt? How long will they refuse to believe in me, in spite of all the miraculous signs I have performed among them? I will strike them down with a plague and destroy them, but I will make you into a nation greater and stronger than they."
>
> Numbers 14:11-13

Moses told the Lord that the Egyptians would hear about it, and he reminded God that it was by His power these people were brought out from among them (v. 14).

The following verses tell us Moses began begging God to spare the people. Do not miss this: *Moses was praying*. Moses was praying for those people. Why was he praying for them? Well, God had said He was going to destroy them. That is a pretty good reason to pray for somebody, isn't it?

Remember what happened. The children of Israel were poised for greatness. They were on the edge of the Promised Land. Moses sent out twelve spies who were to scout the territory and return with a plan and say, "This is what we need to do to conquer the land."

They did not do that. They returned, and two of them said, "Let's go and take this land like God said."

Ten of them said, "We will not succeed."

The people voted and the majority said, "Oh, no, we can't do that!" They agreed with the ten that were negative.

They said to God, "Oh, God, you said we can do it, and God, you said we should do it, but we took a vote and the majority said, 'We are not going to do it.' "

And God said, "Oh, that is okay, the majority rules, and I am happy with it."

No! God did not say that. God said, "Moses, stand back. I am going to destroy this people." And Moses began to pray for them. He talked to God, and he prayed for the people.

We want to concentrate now on praying for other people. Often you hear this referred to as intercession. That is a beautiful word, *intercession*. Literally, it means *to go before royalty on behalf of someone else.*

Sometimes when a person is sentenced for execution, another goes in his place to the governor or to the President to ask for a reprieve. Praying for other people is like that. It is going before God Almighty on their behalf, asking for mercy and pardon. That is a neat concept, isn't it?

Often we say, "I will pray for you." Praying for someone means I will plead your case with God. I will talk to God on your behalf. I will put my hand in God's hand and my hand in your hand to bring you together. That is powerful, isn't it? What is praying for other people? It is interceding. It is going to royalty on behalf of another person.

We need to pray for people. This is not a *maybe*. This is not a *should we*. We truly need to pray for other people.

REASONS TO PRAY FOR OTHER PEOPLE

People have problems. They always will. Some problems just come from the circumstances of everyday life. Some problems people make for themselves. Let me give you a couple of reasons we need to pray for other people.

OTHER PEOPLE NEED OUR PRAYERS
We should pray for other people because they need our prayers. Very simply, they need them.

Moses' people needed to be prayed for. They needed it. If God came to me this evening or He came to someone else and said He was going to strike you down, you would want to be prayed for, true? Moses prayed for his people because they needed it, and we should pray for people because they need it. You and I need it. We all need someone to pray for us.

Several years ago, George Barna, a Christian pollster, released studies that showed the divorce rate among born-again Christians is almost the same as for non-Christians, and it is still hovering around forty-five to fifty percent. Four out of ten marriages end in divorce. Why should we pray for people? We should pray for them because they need it. In the last thirty years, teen suicide in America has tripled. Why should you and I pray for the people in our lives? They need it.

PRAY FOR OTHER PEOPLE BECAUSE YOU LOVE THEM

Another reason we pray for others is because Christians are to be people of love. Why should I pray for you? Why should you pray for me? It ought to come from who you are.

At the end of his prayer, Moses said, "God, in accordance with Your great love, forgive the sin of this people. God, pardon them just as you have pardoned them in the past" (*Author's paraphrase*). Moses was appealing to God's love, but Moses was praying for those people because *he* loved them.

Why should you pray for people? Pray for them because *you* love them. My lack of prayer for you or yours for me or others may stem from a bitter heart. When we love people like we should, praying for them is a natural thing.

PRAY FOR OTHER PEOPLE JUST AS JESUS DID

We need to pray for other people as we follow the example set by Jesus Christ. Moses, David, Paul, and many others in Scripture are examples of men who prayed on behalf of others. The Bible says Jesus even now sits at the right hand of the Father interceding for us.

First John 2:6 tells me that if I am in Christ I am to be like Jesus. Everything Jesus did is my pattern and my goal for the way I am to live. Do you know why I should pray for you? I should pray for you because my Lord set that as a standard. Jesus prayed for people. I should pray for you, you should pray for me, and we should pray for others because we are following Jesus' example. That's a great thing.

NOT TO PRAY FOR OTHERS IS SINFUL

A particularly important reason to pray for others is that it is sinful not to pray for people. If Moses had not prayed for his people, that would have been sinful. First Samuel 12:23 is a great little verse, "Far be it from me that I should sin against the Lord by failing to pray for you." That is powerful, isn't it? When we neglect to pray for people we ought to be praying for, that is not just missing a great opportunity; it is sinful.

The best reason I have heard for why we should pray for others is the same reason you would throw a drowning man a rope. The drowning man needs it. If you have any kind of a heart, you will want to do it. Good people certainly would do it, and you would be a scoundrel not to.

Why should I pray for other people? Why should you? Several reasons are that they need it and that you have Jesus and love in your heart. Why am I going to pray for people? I am going to pray for them because other good people and Jesus Christ have set that example for me and because it is sinful not to.

PRAY FOR EVERYONE IN YOUR LIFE

For whom should we pray? Moses prayed for the people in his life that desperately needed it. First Timothy 2:1 says: "I urge, then, first of all, that requests, prayers and intercessions and thanksgiving be made for everyone...." That opens it up. Some people you and I should be praying for are our immediate family members, our relatives, our friends, and our enemies. Do you have an enemy prayer list? For whom should we pray? The list is endless.

Let me tell you a way you and I can really improve our ability to pray for people. Take a piece of paper and write down the names of everybody you ought to be praying for. It will astonish you. You may easily come up with fifty to a hundred names.

Let me share with you a system a professor taught us to do that works so well. He said to take that list, let's say you have a hundred names, and divide that by the seven days of the week. Pray every day for your immediate family. Then look at the days of the week and fill in the blanks. Maybe on Sunday you pray for your immediate family and your church staff and missionaries. Monday, pray for your extended family and relatives. Tuesday could be set aside for praying for people at work and Wednesday for people in the neighborhood. You see how this works. I have found if I am organized in this, I accomplish much more.

Make a list of people in your life that need your prayers: cousins you have not seen in thirty years that may not be Christians or people down the street you have never prayed for. Organization will make your prayer life better.

Do you remember the long distance commercial: *Reach out and touch someone?* It is exciting to me that in prayer I can reach out and touch somebody. In fact, in prayer I can reach out and touch people I hardly ever see. I can reach out and touch people that will not ever come to my church, will not let me witness to them, and will not hear a word I have to say. But they cannot control what I do when I am alone with God.

You see, by praying for other people, we can reach out and touch them. We can reach out and touch them for God. For whom should we pray? Pray for everybody you can. The better organized you are, the better you will pray. Nobody is outside your reach.

HOW DO WE PRAY FOR OTHER PEOPLE?

How do we pray effectively for other people?

Pray for Other People with Love

When we pray for other people, first of all, we should pray from a heart of love. Moses said, "God, in accordance with your great love, please, forgive these people." Moses was coming to God because he loved these people, and as he prayed for them he was praying from a heart of love. That is such an important starting point.

PRAY FOR OTHERS LIKE YOU WANT TO BE PRAYED FOR

Something else that will help you pray for other people is to pray for them like you want to be prayed for.

I saw a story about something that is sad, but it is so true. A couple of good church men were talking, and a man named Bob was approaching them. One of the men looked at the other and said, "Oh, my, I told Bob I would pray for him." So he looked up and said, "God, bless Bob."

Bob walked up and the man told him, "Bob, I have been praying for you."

Now, I want to tell you this and it may be a little tough, but I think it is true. We commit a horrible lie when we tell people we are going to pray for them and we don't do it.

When you pray for yourself, is there passion in your prayer? There is for me. I pray with passion when I am praying for myself because I am serious, and when I pray for you with the same intensity I pray with when I am praying for myself, do you know what? I pray for you well.

Matthew 7:12 says: "In everything, do to others as you would have them do to you...." Would that not apply to praying? Do you want to pray better when you pray for other people? Pray for them like you want to be prayed for. That means to take this seriously, spend some time doing it, and pray for them with passion and intensity.

BE SPECIFIC WHEN YOU PRAY FOR OTHER PEOPLE

Another great help in praying for other people is to be as specific as you can. Moses did not say, "Oh, God, just whatever you want to do will be fine." He said, "God, forgive them. God, spare them, please. They do not deserve it, God, but do it for them."

I read a story of a young pastor still in seminary. An elderly lady who befriended him and his wife regularly would ask them, "What should I pray about for you?" She would take out a little notebook and write down his name and the requests, and she would say, "I will be praying for you."

When she would have another occasion to visit with them, she would ask, "What did God do about that?" She would pull out her notebook. Sometimes she would write down, "Keep praying." Sometimes she would write "Praise God, He answered."

What impressed this minister is how specific she was. She was intentional in taking notes and really trying to pray to God specifically for this couple.

Sometimes we cannot be specific. Someone may simply say, "There is a family in our neighborhood that needs prayer. That is all I can tell you." God will honor your prayer for them. When you cannot be specific, God honors that. But be as specific as you can.

Pray for them by name. Pray for them by need. When I pray for people, I picture their face in my mind. Often when I am praying for church members, I use the pictorial directory. That helps me concentrate better and pray better. Be as specific as you can.

PRAY FOR OTHER PEOPLE CONSISTENTLY

Pray for other people consistently. Luke says Jesus told His disciples a parable to teach them they should "always pray and not give up" (18:1). Have you prayed for somebody and you wanted to quit? If you have done much praying, you have.

I want to challenge you to be consistent. Pray for others when they ask you to. Pray for them when their name comes to your mind. Pray for them in your quiet time and throughout the day. Be consistent in lifting them up to God. Pray for them. Pray for them consistently.

WHAT TO PRAY FOR OTHER PEOPLE

What do we pray for other people? A pastor was preaching a children's sermon, and he had all the kids around him. He was talking with them about praying for other people when he asked the kids, "Do your parents ever pray for you?" One little boy, kind of a trouble-maker, raised his hand. The preacher hesitantly asked, "Do your parents pray for you?"

The boy said, "Yes, yes."

Of course, the parents were nervously watching, wondering what he might say.

The preacher asked, "What do they pray for?"

The little boy said, "Every night when Momma tucks me in, she looks up and says, 'Thank God, he's in bed.' "

That is one way you can pray for someone, but let me tell you some better ways.

Pray for Other People with Spiritual Needs

The first is this, and this ought to be the first thing, pray for people about their spiritual issues. It does not do anyone any good to be healed and then to die and go to hell. The number one thing we need to pray about is people coming to Christ, and the number two thing we need to pray about is for Christians to begin living for Christ.

What is keeping the churches back throughout the world is not so much the devil as it is the Christians in the churches and the preachers in the churches. We are the stumbling blocks. We need to pray for other people that their spiritual needs will be met and that people will come to Christ and get their hearts right with Him.

Before I moved to Texas in 1986, I spent some time as interim supply pastor at a little church in Tennessee. There was a wonderful man in that church named Stanley. Stanley was not religiously trained, but he knew his Bible. Better than that, he knew his Lord. Stanley used to talk to me about one of his children. Stanley would say, "I'm praying for her to come to Christ. My daughter is lost, and I want her to be saved." Stanley would tear up, and he would say, "I'm telling God, 'Do whatever you have to do in her life to bring her to salvation.' "

That is a strong prayer. You had better think that through before you pray it. But what my blessed friend understood is this: There is nothing more important than eternity and coming to Jesus Christ. What should we pray for people about? The number one thing to pray for other people is for their spiritual needs.

Pray for Other People about Everything

The second thing to pray for others is to pray for them about everything. Philippians 4:6 says: "Do not worry about anything, but *in everything,* pray. Pray and offer up your requests with thanksgiving" (*Author's paraphrase*).When someone has a need, pray for that need to be met. If they are taking a test, pray for them to do well on that test. We should pray for people about everything that is a specific need in their life at the time.

The children of Israel had one specific need at that time, didn't they? The need was for God not to destroy them. That is what Moses was praying for, wasn't it? He was saying, "God, please do not do to them what they deserve and what you want to do to them."

What do you pray for people about? Certainly, pray for spiritual things, but also pray for everything of concern in their lives: physical, emotional, financial. Whatever affects their life, you pray for them about that.

THERE IS GREAT POWER IN PRAYING FOR OTHER PEOPLE

There is great power in praying for other people. In Numbers 14:13-19, Moses was praying to God. Now look in verse twenty. "The Lord replied, 'I have forgiven them as you have asked.' "

God punished them, but He did not kill them as He had intended. And the only thing we can deduct from this story if we take the Bible as truth is that God heard Moses' prayer, and He intervened, and He responded, and He turned away. People were going to be destroyed, and a man just like you and me went before God and said, "God, please, do not do that." And God said, "Okay."

James 5:16 is a tremendous verse that talks about Elijah's prayer, the prayer of a righteous and powerful man. The Old Testament story is about Elijah doing battle with evil men. Elijah prayed that it would not rain for three and a half years, and it did not rain. Then Elijah prayed for rain, and it rained (v. 17-18).

What makes this story so full of hope for us is that James says about Elijah, "He was a person just like us." Elijah was not any more special to God than you and I are. The power that was available to Elijah in prayer is available to us. There is power in praying for other people. There always has been.

In the late 1980s, Dr. Randolph Byrd, a cardiologist at San Francisco General Hospital in California, did an experiment with 393 heart patients he separated into two groups. He assigned some people to pray for the patients in one of the groups. All they knew is they were praying on a first-name basis for a person who had heart problems. The other group was not prayed for.

Ten months later, the group that had been prayed for was five times less likely to be on antibiotics, less likely to have suffered a cardiac arrest, and less likely to have been in congestive heart failure.[1] Do you believe those people would say it had an effect on their lives when someone prayed for them?

In 1998, I had a seriously ill church member in the intensive care unit in a hospital in Abilene, Texas. I visited with her and the family several times, but then I had to go out of town. It looked as if she were going to die, so they called the chairman of my deacon body, a man named Delbert Schaefer. They said, "Delbert, will you go see the family and pray for them?"

Delbert went to the ICU unit. When he walked in, the doctor was with the family telling them, "She has a two percent chance to live." The family looked at Delbert, and they asked, "Will you, please, pray for her?"

Delbert took them by the hands and began to pray. He said, "God, we are in a hopeless situation, but You are God, and I am asking You to heal this lady. God, I've prayed before and some have died and some have lived. God, I am asking you to heal this lady."

Six weeks later, she was in church. God used an humble and good Christian man's prayers to extend this lady's life. God used his prayer. The same God that heard his prayer and Elijah's prayer is the same God available to us. There is power in praying for other people.

MAKE A DECISION TO PRAY FOR OTHER PEOPLE

Christian, are you an intercessor? Don't say, "Praying for other people is not my gift." God wants us to pray for other people. Make a commitment to be a man or woman who consistently, systematically, and wholeheartedly prays for other people.

Do you want to pray well for other people?
Do your want to tap into God's power for them?
Pray with us, and see God work. www.fbcruston.org

7

WHAT DOES THE BIBLE SAY ABOUT PRAYING FOR OURSELVES

Several years ago in the *Ft. Worth Star-Telegram,* there was a sad story about a forty-five year old man who was leaving his job on Friday afternoon as he had done many, many times before. In fact, he had worked for this company twenty years, but this Friday things were a little different. He had just left a meeting where he had been told he was one of two hundred people who would be losing their jobs in a month. Forty-five years old, he was going home to a wife and three small kids. Without much formal education, without much savings in the bank, and with a lot of bills; here was a man who had a desperate situation.

What should he do? Well, there probably were a lot of things he could have done and should have done. One thing he needed desperately to do was to pray.

I want us to look at a part of prayer I really think is misunderstood, and that is praying for ourselves. Prayer is such a great subject; it is inexhaustible. Now I want us to think about praying for ourselves.

PRAYING FOR OURSELVES

One question we need to answer properly is whether it is okay to pray for ourselves.

I heard a seminary professor make a statement that to me was very odd. He said he did not pray for himself. He said he used that time praying for other people, and he did not pray for himself. When he said that, there was a slight glow on his face, and honestly, this statement made him look good and noble.

But after class some of the students began to talk and we thought, you know, he needs to pray for himself. He is kind of grouchy. He is not real friendly. He does not have a very vibrant personality. A little prayer might help him, but he had implied that praying for ourselves was selfish and that it may not be a good thing to do.

In the year 2001, an interesting little book, *The Prayer of Jabez*[1], was published. You may have read that book. I think it was a fantastic book. It was based on 1 Chronicles 4:10. The prayer of that book was from an Old Testament character named Jabez who said, "God, bless me, protect me, and enlarge my borders."

The book sold millions of copies. But after it was published, other books were published refuting that book, saying how bad it was, how selfish it was. My response to that is no, it was not selfish. No, it was not a wrong prayer because God answered his prayer. God does not answer wrong prayers.

PRAYING FOR OURSELVES IS A RIGHT THING TO DO

I want to establish a simple but important truth: it is okay to pray for ourselves. The problem is that some people pray *only* for themselves. They do not pray for other people, they do not spend time thanking God or praising God or getting their hearts right. All they do is pray, "God, give me, give me, help me, help me." And, of course, we know that is childish at best, wrong at worst. But let me tell you, praying for yourself is a proper thing for you to do.

JESUS TAUGHT US TO PRAY FOR OURSELVES

Jesus, in teaching the disciples how to pray and teaching you and me how to pray said, "Give us today our daily bread" (Matt. 6:11).

72

Jesus was teaching His followers and us to pray for ourselves. Now, if we need to establish a pattern for our guide, *what Jesus taught* says it is okay to pray for ourselves.

JESUS PRAYED FOR HIMSELF

What Jesus did shows us it is okay to pray for ourselves. When Jesus was in the Garden of Gethsemane, He was not praying that Pilate would be a better person, was He? He was not praying that King Herod would repent and become moral. For whom He was praying? He was praying for Himself (Matt. 26:36-45).

Jesus did not do anything wrong. In fact, we are told that as Christians we are to imitate Christ (1 John 2:6). Jesus prayed for Himself. Praying for ourselves is following Jesus' example.

SCRIPTURE TEACHES US TO PRAY FOR OURSELVES

Paul said he prayed three times that God would remove the thorn in his flesh (2 Cor. 12:8). What did Paul do? He prayed for himself. Praying for ourselves is a good thing to do. It is positive, and it is biblical. It is a right thing to do.

The problem with a lot of teachings and writings on prayer is they can sound very spiritual and yet not be based in Scripture. Always base your understanding of God and God's principles on examples from the Bible. It is good and right to pray for ourselves.

WHY SHOULD WE PRAY FOR OURSELVES?

Why should we pray for ourselves? Let me give you some very good answers.

WE NEED PRAYER

We should pray for ourselves because we need it. "Give us today our daily bread" (Matt. 6:11). The bread Jesus mentioned here was a necessity. He was talking about what these people needed. He knew they had needs they needed to ask God to meet.

You and I do, too. We have needs we need to ask God to meet. Should you ask someone else to pray for you? Surely, you should.

Should you get your spouse, boyfriend or girlfriend, or your best friend to pray for you? Certainly, but there are needs you have I hope you do not share with anybody but God. You pray for yourself from your own basis of needs.

PRAYER HELPS US DEPEND ON GOD

Prayer helps us depend on God. Jesus said pray, "Give us today our daily bread." Jesus is constantly trying to get us to depend on God. He always tries to get us to get off self and to depend on God.

I heard Max Lucado, the great Christian writer and preacher from San Antonio, Texas, say that when he neglects prayer, his preaching becomes weaker, his writing becomes weaker, and his ability to help others is greatly reduced. Lucado clearly implied he has less power without prayer, and he went on to say the act of praying helps him continually depend on God.

That is so true. Praying not only helps me reach greater heights, it reminds me the only way I can reach greater heights is by God.

Do you know why a lot of churches and individuals are so flat? They stopped depending on God. Prayer causes us to depend on God. It causes us to reach out more and more. That is a huge goal of the Christian life.

Humanly speaking, the goal of life is to become independent. You are born dependent, and your parents hope at some point when you become an adult you will get a job and move out of the house. That is a goal.

Spiritually, the goal is just the opposite. We are spiritually independent when we come to Christ, and the goal is to become more and more dependent. Serious prayer helps us become more dependent on God. One reason we should pray for ourselves is it shows us our need for dependence on God and helps us develop that dependence.

We pray for ourselves because we need help beyond just our own ability. Why do you exercise? Why do you go on a diet? You need help. Why do you pray for yourself? You need help. You want God to help you.

GOD WORKS THROUGH PRAYER

We pray for ourselves because prayer is the way God has chosen to work. Do not fall for the deception, "God knows my needs; therefore, I do not need to ask." That is not biblical. Even though it sounds spiritual, it is not right. James tells us we do not have because we do not ask (4:2). God says, "Yes, I know your needs. I know, but I want you to ask."

Does God do things without our asking? Absolutely, but let me remind you of Billy Graham's words. Billy Graham said he believes when we get to heaven God is going to show us a room with all the wonderful answers to prayers we could have had if we had just asked. I do not think that is far-fetched.

Why should you pray for yourself? You should pray for yourself because prayer is a huge way God has chosen to work. To not pray for yourself, to not ask for yourself means there will be things you will never receive because God has chosen to work through our prayers.

HOW DO YOU PRAY FOR YOURSELF?

How do we pray for ourselves? What are some simple principles we need to abide by when we pray for ourselves?

PRAY CONSISTENTLY

The first principle in praying effectively for yourself is to pray consistently. Jesus said, "Give us today our yearly bread?" No. He said, "Give us our daily bread" (Matt. 6:11). Jesus taught that prayer ought to be a consistent thing in our life.

Praying consistently is a key. I do not know how many times I have heard and you must have heard it said, "I prayed about that for several days and nothing happened. Prayer does not work." That is a wrong conclusion. God says a fundamental key to prayer is staying with it. A key to making your prayer life effective when you pray for yourself is to pray and continue to pray.

E. M. Bounds was a great preacher in the 1800s who devoted the last part of his life to writing on prayer. He has some books on prayer that, in my opinion, are timeless. They would be wonderful for you to read sometime. Bounds made the statement that prayer is the greatest thing we can do, but he went on to make the point that it demands time and attention, that prayer is not something we can just carelessly rush into. It must be our top priority. How true those words are!

And we are going, "God bless the day, and bless this, and bless this. I am in my car. I am on my cell phone. And every now and then I am praying." That is okay. You can do that. But you also need to set aside some time you devote just to being alone with God and talking with Him in prayer. You need to be consistent about doing that.

PRAY WITH PURE MOTIVES

Another key principle for how you pray for yourself is to pray with pure motives. James tells us this: "When you ask, you do not receive because you ask with wrong motives ..." (4:3). Some of us do not receive what we pray for because we do not ask. We do not feel the need or we are too lazy to pray. Some of us ask and do not receive because our motives are wrong.

Now this is tough. How do we pray and ask God to help us financially? How do we ask Him to help us at work to get a promotion, or to get a raise, or to get a better job? How do we ask God to help us in those areas without having impure motives?

The only thing I can tell you is check your own heart. One thing I pray to God on a regular basis is, "God, help me with my motives. God, show me where my motives are wrong. God, purify my motives." I think that is an important part of prayer because this gets into a gray area sometimes, doesn't it? "God, please move my boss to a company in Alaska." Okay, check your heart on that. God may end up moving you if you pray that enough. He may solve the problem. Sometimes when you pray, you need to ask God to help you with your motives.

PRAY FOR YOUR NEEDS INSTEAD OF YOUR WANTS

When you pray for yourself, a guiding principle you always should follow is to be careful not to confuse your needs and your wants. When He taught us to pray "Give us today our daily bread"

(Matt. 6:11) Jesus was talking about needs. This becomes confusing because you know God wants to bless you. If you have walked with Christ very long, you know God has not just met your needs. He has blessed you, hasn't He? He blesses you far beyond your needs.

There may be times in your Christian walk when He meets just your needs and you have to take one day at a time, but as you continue to walk with Christ He blesses you, doesn't He? But be careful about praying for the Corvette if you have a decent car. Be careful about praying to win the lottery. Let me remind you more than a million other people are praying that same prayer just as fervently as you are every week. Be careful about confusing the need and the want.

Some of us are disappointed because God does not give us our every want. He does not promise us that. He does promise to bless us, and He promises to meet our needs. "My God shall supply all my needs" (Phil. 4:19). Prayer is the way we ask to get those needs met.

I heard a beautiful story of a pastor lecturing on prayer. They had a question-and-answer time, and one of the men raised his hand and said, "Preacher, tell me in basic terms, how do I pray for myself?"

The preacher smiled, and he said, "Ask God."

Ask Him with a pure heart. Ask Him consistently. Be careful not to confuse your needs and your wants, but just ask Him. Ask Him.

WHAT DO YOU PRAY FOR YOURSELF?

When you pray for yourself, what do you pray for? What requests of your own does God want you to bring to Him?

PRAY FOR YOUR NEEDS

When you pray for yourself, pray for your needs: "Give us today our daily bread." In the ancient East where Jesus lived, bread was the staple of their diet. This was not asking for Grandmomma's special dinner rolls with honey butter. This was saying, "God meet my most basic need for food."

Almost every Bible scholar says when Jesus said, "Give us our daily bread," He was not talking just about food. He was talking about our needs. He was talking about what we need in life.

Dr. John MacArthur, a pastor in California, said this prayer applies to many of us who need to say, "God, help me avoid the bread at the meal."[2] That may sound surprising, but I think it is true. Some of us as we pray for our needs should pray not, "God, give me my daily bread" but, "God, keep the bread away from me. Please, God, help me there."

Martin Luther, the great Christian scholar in the 1500s, said when Jesus talked here about bread, this was symbolic of everything necessary to life—our health, our food, the weather when a storm is coming up, our bodies, our family, everything.

St. Augustine said this passage was talking about all of our soul and body needs. When Jesus says, "God, give us our daily bread," he is talking about things necessary for life. That may be food. It may be money. It may be health. Pray for all of your needs. Go to God for those things.

Pray for Your Spiritual Development

Pray for your spiritual development when you pray for yourself. One thing you and I need to pray hard about is "God, help me to be a more dedicated Christian." When was the last time you said, "Jesus, help me hunger and thirst after you more; Jesus, help me love you more; help me fall more in love with praying and studying my Bible"? When you pray for yourself, pray diligently for your spiritual development.

Pray for Your Personal Development

Pray for personal development in your life. A friend of mine was well-intended, but again, I think he knew more theory than fact about some things. I heard him say a couple of times, "Don't ever pray for patience." He was very serious. He said if you pray for patience, God will put something in your life to make you have to become patient.

I thought: that is one of the craziest things I have ever heard. That is like saying if you pray to be more loving God may put some irritating person in your life to make you more loving.

Should you pray for patience? Absolutely, you should. Should you pray to be more loving and kind? Surely, you should. Pray for personality issues in your life. Absolutely, pray for those things.

PRAY FOR EVERYTHING IN YOUR LIFE

Pray for everything in your life. Jesus said through Paul, "Don't worry about anything, but instead, in everything," do what? You pray (Phil. 4:6). "Cast all your cares upon Him" (I Peter 5:7). How do you cast cares on God? You cast your cares on God in prayer.

What should you pray for in your life? Pray for everything, spiritual things and personal things. You pray for everything in your life.

One preacher who had just finished seminary and was very proud of the degree he had earned was praying in his new church. He began to ramble on as he had several weeks in a row at prayer meeting, saying, "We beseech Thee in Thy benevolence to bestow Thy blessings on these believers." He continued with the high-sounding talk several minutes until someone on the front row said, "Preacher, shut up, and just ask God for something."

I do not encourage you to do that at prayer meeting, but I do encourage you when you are praying for anybody, especially for yourself, do it without the pious-sounding religious language. Just ask God. Ask God for everything you need, and in every area of your life ask Him to take care of you.

DOES PRAYING FOR OURSELVES REALLY MATTER?

Does praying for ourselves matter? Jesus said pray, "Give us today our daily needs" (*Author's paraphrase*). Does it matter? Let me share with you a few stories where I know it mattered.

Before I became a Christian, twenty-five years ago, I had been living very far away from what was right, but because of my upbringing I knew right from wrong. I had been an active part of a crowd that mainly partied and lived completely opposite to the way God wanted us to live.

When I became a Christian, I knew if I were going to walk for Jesus my mouth had to straighten up. I knew I could not go out and drink a twelve-pack of beer Friday night because those guys knew drunkenness and God didn't go together, and I didn't know how I was going to do it.

But the very night I got saved, later I got back down on my knees, and I said, "God, I don't know how this is going to work, but You have to help me in two areas. God, You have to clean up my mouth, and You have to get the beer out of my hands, and I don't think I can do it, God." But do you know what? God miraculously answered that prayer. And I have struggled with a million things since then, but I found out right at the beginning—praying for myself mattered.

One of my dear friends in seminary came from a wonderful family, but it was a family that could not help him very much financially. He was pastoring a church and going to school full time, and he just did not have any money. My friend was in dire straits. Now, he is pastoring and doing well. God has blessed him faithfully. But I will always remember when we were in seminary he would tell me, "Man, I don't know if I am going to make it financially, but I am going to keep praying and asking God to meet my needs."

Now, he is very well-blessed in every area of his life. But what he found out as a young Christian was that God would meet those needs he kept pleading with Him to meet. God was faithful, and He met his needs.

Does praying for yourself work? Absolutely. If you are a born-again Christian trying to be right with others and right with God, when you go to God for yourself, absolutely, it works. Jesus said:

Ask and it will be given to you; seek and you will find; knock and the door will be opened to you. For everyone who asks receives; he who seeks finds; and to him who knocks, the door will be opened.

Matthew 7:7-8

That applies to your praying for yourself as much as for anything else. Isn't that wonderful? Does praying for yourself work? Yes, it does.

A daddy was looking out of his kitchen window one afternoon at his little boy playing in the sandbox, and he noticed the son was struggling to get a big rock out of the sandbox. The child worked on that rock trying to roll it and lift it, and he could not get it out. Finally, he kicked the rock, which is never a positive thing to do. He hurt his stubby, little toes, and then he just sat down and began to pout.

The daddy went out, and he put his arm around the boy, and he said, "Son, you couldn't move the rock, could you?"

"No, sir."

"You want the rock out of your sandbox, don't you?"

"Yes, sir."

"Son, did you use all the strength you could use to you to get that rock out of the sandbox?"

"Yes, sir."

"Son, did you use all the strength available to you to get that rock out?"

"Yes, sir."

"No, you didn't. You didn't ask your father."

The daddy leaned down, picked up the rock, and set it out of the sandbox.

You know when I read that story, I thought: Oh, my goodness. How many rocks are in my sandbox I just have not asked the Father to pick up?

Are you struggling with sin you have not asked God to help you with? Are you struggling with hurts and pain you have not asked God to remove and have not really wanted Him to?

Sometimes we say, "I just don't witness very well. That is not who I am," but we have not spent time praying and asking God to break our heart for lost people and to make us a witness. We say, "It's a struggle praying," but we have never bothered to ask the Father to help us pray. You see, there are always going to be things in our sandboxes we can't get out, but we have a Father who can.

PRAY FOR YOURSELF

Christian, I want to challenge you to be a man or woman who prays for yourself diligently and fervently the rest of your life. Commit to pray for yourself.

Maybe you are away from God and that very fact has limited your ability to be effective in prayer, and you need to come back to God. You come back to Him.

Maybe God has been dealing with your heart about your relationship with Jesus. Maybe you don't have one. That is why prayer has always seemed so hard and distant. You need to give your life to Jesus.

Let me tell you, whatever it is you need to do, respond to Christ's call on your life.

Do you know what it means to be truly loved and forgiven?
Jesus wants that for you, and He will do it for you.
Pour out your heart to Him when you pray for yourself.
See how to be saved at www.fbcruston.org

8

WHAT IS PRAYING IN FAITH ALL ABOUT

When you think of prayer, what are some things that come to your mind? Perhaps you associate prayer and food; you ask God to bless your food. In the old days, we associated prayer with a ball game. We had a ballgame, we prayed. Maybe you think about praying only when you are in trouble and want God to help you.

When you think about prayer, do you ever think about the word *faith?*

FAITH IS FUNDAMENTAL TO CHRISTIANITY

And without faith it is impossible to please God, because anyone who comes to him must believe that he exists and that he rewards those who earnestly seek him.   Hebrews 11:6

You were Saved by Faith
You were saved by faith in Christ. Your part of salvation is responding to God's grace through faith. "For it is by grace you have you have been saved, through faith" (Eph. 2:8).

You Continue the Christian Life by Faith

You continue to live the Christian life by that faith in God, that trust in God, and that commitment to God all wrapped up in that one word *faith*. Saved by faith, we continue to walk in Jesus Christ in faith.

It is Impossible to Please God without Faith

It is impossible to please God without faith. You are saved by it, you live by it, and you cannot please God without it. You and I can never please God or make God happy without faith in God.

That is also true in our human relationships. I remember talking with a young lady about her relationship with her boyfriend.

"He does not trust anything I do. Does that make me happy? Absolutely not," she said. "I am miserable."

As we talked further, I understood he had a lot of reasons not to trust her, but her fundamental premise was correct. You cannot be happy without faith, and it is impossible to please God without faith. Faith is vital to pleasing God.

FAITH IS A KEY TO ANSWERED PRAYER

Faith is a Key to Prayer

Faith is a key to prayer. "Whatever you ask for in prayer, believe that you have received it, and it will be yours" (Mark 11:24). Faith in God is a key to answered prayer, but there are several keys. You cannot build your prayer life on just one; you have to build it on all of these keys.

You Have to Be Born Again

You have to be born again. You have to be saved. If you desire for God to hear your prayers, you must have a relationship with Him.

You Must Be Living for Jesus

As a Christian, you must be walking with Jesus. You must have a good relationship and live in fellowship with Jesus Christ. Remember, Jesus promised, "If you abide in me and my words abide in you, *then* you may ask, and *then* I will hear" (John 15:7, *Author's paraphrase*). You need to be saved, and you need to be living for Jesus.

YOU MUST FORGIVE OTHER PEOPLE

Your heart needs to be right with other people. You and I cannot be bitter, unforgiving Christians and expect to connect with God in prayer.

All these keys really are essential to connecting properly with God in prayer. Let me illustrate this with our office building. It takes three keys to get into my office. I use one key to get into the building, another key to get in the office suite, and I use that last key to open the door to my personal office. Three separate keys are essential for me to get into my office. If I have only two of those keys, I am effectively locked out of my office.

I have heard people say, "Faith is the key to prayer." It is *one* of the keys to prayer. Being saved is a key. Living right with Christ is another, and having a heart right with other people is one more. Each of those things is absolutely essential for us to connect properly with God.

If you want to see things happen when you pray, you need faith. You must have that belief and trust in God. John Calvin, the Reformation theologian, reportedly said the door to prayer cannot be unlocked without faith. That is an accurate statement. You can have everything else right, but without faith the door to prayer cannot be unlocked.

HOW DO WE PRAY IN FAITH?

How do we pray in faith? Praying in faith begins with believing you are talking to God when you pray. Faith believes you are connecting with God. "And without faith it is impossible to please God, because anyone who comes to him must believe that he exists..." (Heb. 11:6).

BELIEVE YOU ARE TALKING WITH GOD

When you pray, are you really conscious of the fact you are trying to connect with God Almighty? Are you just saying the Lord's Prayer before you go to bed, just saying a rote prayer, reading a prayer, or sending up something to heaven, hoping something happens? If you are, you are wasting your breath.

Praying in faith begins with the clear belief that when you pray you are connecting with God Almighty, that God is there. Anyone who comes to Him must believe He exists. That may sound fundamental. It is fundamental. It is fundamental to success in your prayer life.

BELIEVE GOD IS LISTENING AND THAT HE CARES

Praying in faith is believing God is listening and that God cares. When you pray, do you really believe God is hearing you and that He cares about what you are discussing with Him?

This is a part of faith because sometimes you are not going to feel this. This is not a feeling; this is faith. Sometimes you are not going to sense emotionally that God is there and that He is tuning in to you. Sometimes you feel that; sometimes you do not. Praying in faith is believing God exists, believing He is there, believing He listens, and believing He cares.

In Jesus and Paul's day, many of the religious systems professed multiple gods, and they believed those gods did not care for humanity, that mankind just got in their way. Christianity is built on this: There is one God who deeply and intimately cares about you. Faith believes He rewards those who earnestly seek him (Heb. 11:6).

When you approach God in prayer, do you believe He is there? Do you believe He really cares about you? That is the basis of praying in faith, the fundamental requirement for praying in faith.

BELIEVE GOD CAN DO WHAT YOU ASK

Praying in faith believes God can do what you are asking Him to do. Do you really believe God can do what you ask Him to do? I think most people don't.

Epicureus, a Stoic philosopher of Jesus and Paul's day, listed as a first principle of Stoicism: God does nothing. Imagine how terrible it would be going through life having as the first principle of your philosophy that God does nothing.

One of the principles of faith is God can do things and God does do things. "Whatever you ask for in prayer, believe that you have received it, and it will be yours" (Mark 11:24). Luke 18:27 is a great verse that says, "What is impossible with men is possible with God."

When you approach God to pray for yourself or for other people, to pray for your church or for your world; please, approach God in faith believing He is there, believing He is listening to you, believing He cares, and by all means believe He can do what you are asking Him to do, or do not waste your time.

Prayer is not a superstitious act. It will not benefit you or God or anyone else just to say some words before you go to sleep, hoping something happens. Faith is not wishing something is going to happen. Faith is believing God is hearing you, and it is believing God can do what you are asking Him to do for you.

Believe God Will Do What You Ask

Praying in faith not only believes God can but God will do what you are asking Him to do.

Years ago, a minister in Scotland was walking with one of his parishioners. The man had a lot of problems, and as they walked the preacher said, "I have been telling you to pray. Are you praying about these problems?"

The man said, "Yes, but nothing much has happened."

The preacher looked back at him and asked, "Do you expect much to happen?"

And the man said, "No, I really don't."

The preacher answered, "That is one of the major reasons nothing has been happening when you pray. You do not expect much to happen." Praying in faith is believing not only that God *can* but that God *will* do what you ask.

In West Texas, the story is told that in one of the many droughts they experience some farmers gathered weekly in their fields to pray for relief from their desperate situation. One man drove by every week and saw the farmers praying.

Finally, he stopped one day, and he said, "What are you guys doing?" He knew what they were doing.

They said, "We are praying for rain."

"Do you really believe God is going to send rain?"

"Well, yeah, we believe it."

And the man said, "I don't believe you believe it."

They asked, "Why not?"

And he said, "Where are your umbrellas?"

Praying in faith for rain may involve bringing an umbrella or two. Praying in faith means you believe God hears your prayers and that He can and will do what you ask of Him.

SEE THE ANSWER BEFORE IT HAPPENS

"I tell you, whatever you ask for in prayer, believe that you have received it," believe you already have it, "and it will be yours" (Mark 11:24). Praying in faith means when I pray I believe God is here, and I believe He is hearing me. I believe so firmly He can do and will do what I ask of Him that I can actually see it before it happens.

Faith is being certain of what I do not see (Heb. 11:1). Faith is seeing what has not yet happened. Faith is putting eyes to something before it takes place, seeing it before it happens. I want to share with you a couple of stories I think illustrate so well this concept of praying in faith.

In 1983, I was a young Christian. I had read this Scripture and I had read some good sermons on this subject. I had heard good sermons about praying and believing, but it was hard to practice because praying in faith requires us to trust God totally.

One Sunday afternoon in late November, I came home from college for a day. I was the only one home, and one of our cows got out of the pasture. Now, if you have ever raised cows or worked with cows, you will understand the situation. I had spent as many as five hours chasing one cow. We didn't have horses or four-wheelers, so when a cow got out somebody had to chase it until it was back in the pasture. And every time I got up to this cow to push it back in the gate, it would take off the other way.

Then I thought, why don't you pray? That's a novel idea; I think I'll do it. Why don't you pray in faith?

This may sound silly to you. If you have never chased a cow, it will; if you have chased a cow, it won't. I stopped and quoted this verse to God. "Faith is being certain of what I do not see." And I said, "God, I'm going to believe that cow is going to get back in the pasture." I said, "I don't know how it is going to happen, but by faith I am seeing that cow jump over the fence back into the pasture where it belongs."

And do you know what happened? Within two minutes, the cow walked toward the fence and then jumped over it and was back in the pasture. You may say, "That is silly." I do not think it was silly. I believe God answered my prayer. I saw it before it happened, and then it happened. If you have never chased a cow, you will think it is nonsense; if you have chased a cow, you know as well as I do that it was an answered prayer.

A neat story happened at our university a few months after that. I had a friend who was an exchange student. His student visa was suddenly going to expire a year-and-a-half early. There had been a mistake, and he was going to have to return to Europe. It would be a terrible mess that would be financially costly to him, and it might have caused him to miss a semester or two of school.

We began to pray, and we said, "God, we are going to believe You for a miracle." And, miraculously and mysteriously, within two weeks his visa problems were solved.

Do you remember Jessica Lynch, the young American soldier? On March 23, 2003, she was in Iraq with her unit. They were overrun by a group of Iraqis, and she was taken prisoner. We all believed she was going to die. We were hearing they were doing terrible things to prisoners, but the people in her hometown in West Virginia were praying for her. On April 1, many people were really praying for her, and on that day she was miraculously rescued from a hospital in Iraq and brought back to safety.

Reporters interviewed the Christian principal at her high school, and he said some neat things. He said they had been praying and were expecting her to come back. He went on to say they were already planning the parade for her even before she was found.[1] That is praying in faith. Planning a parade for someone who has not yet been rescued is praying in faith, isn't it?

This is praying in faith—it is believing God hears us, believing He cares, and believing He can and will help.

ACCEPT GOD'S ANSWERS THANKFULLY

Now, let me give you one last extremely important thought on prayer in faith. Praying in faith accepts God's answers thankfully. This is a hard but realistic part of it. Praying in faith accepts God's answers thankfully.

WHEN YOUR PRAYERS ARE UNANSWERED

Sometimes you pray in faith and you believe it. You see the cow jumping back in the pasture or you plan the parade and it doesn't happen, and it breaks your heart, and it should. Why does it not happen? Let me give you a couple of thoughts.

YOU MUST BE RIGHT WITH GOD

When your prayers are unanswered, it may be you are not right with God. You can pray in faith all day but if your heart is away from God, you are bouncing your prayers off the ceiling. If you are bitter or resentful, you are bouncing them off the ceiling; not a Christian, bouncing them off the ceiling.

BELIEVE EVEN WHEN YOU DO NOT UNDERSTAND

Sometimes you can pray in faith as a Christian and to the best of your knowledge your heart is right with other people, you are seeking to be right with God, and you pray in faith, but you do not get what you have been believing for. You do not get what you have been seeing in prayer. Why that is so, I don't know.

Do you know the name Arthur Blessitt? Arthur Blessitt is a dynamic Christian you may remember as the man who carried a cross around the world. He literally walked around the world carrying a large wooden cross.

In several of his speaking engagements, Arthur Blessitt talked about some of his tremendous experiences. He told about coming in contact two days in a row with blind people who were brought to him when he was walking in Africa. The people asked him, "Brother Blessit, will you pray that God will heal this one?"

Arthur said the first day this happened he laid hands on the person and prayed, and he said, "Lord, I believe you are going to heal this person," and the blind person was healed.

He said the very next day in another village, the same scenario happened except when he prayed the person was not healed. He said he cried and he begged God. He pleaded with God, but the person was not healed. Blessitt said, "I don't have an answer for that, but I know I have to keep praying in faith."

This experience has probably been true for you as it has for me. I have prayed for people who were deathly ill, and they have been healed. I have prayed with the same amount of faith for other people to be healed, and I have seen them die. I do not understand that. But praying in faith says, "God, even when I do not understand, I am going to keep trusting you."

In 2 Corinthians 12, Paul tells us a great theological story. The apostle says he prayed three times, "God, remove this thorn in my flesh," and he was not healed.

Paul was a man God used to heal people. Paul did not have a problem with faith. Lack of faith was not his problem with the thorn. Being wrong with God or wrong with others was not his problem. Paul did not have a faith problem. But for whatever reason, God's answer to Paul's praying in faith was, "No, Paul, but my grace will take care of you, and you will know in the by and by why I did not answer the way you wanted me to" (2 Cor. 12:7-9, *Author's paraphrase*).

I am telling you this not to discourage you but because I want you to know you have to pray in faith to see God answer your prayers. You may pray in faith ten times. Eight times out of ten you may see some great results, but there may be those two times you do not. I cannot explain why that happens. But I know if you are praying without faith, you need not expect it to happen because faith is a critical key to prayer.

Let God sort out why some prayers are answered the way we want them to be and some are not. Let God sort that out, and you just keep trusting Him and praying in faith. You know God is not going to honor your prayers if they are not prayed in faith. And you know the best prayers that have ever been prayed are those that have been prayed trusting God before they saw an answer.

GOD RESPONDS TO PRAYERS PRAYED IN FAITH

Hudson Taylor is one of the heroes of the Christian faith. He was a missionary to China, and the story is told that he was on a ship, which would have been a sailboat, that had drifted for days because there was no wind. It began to drift to an island notorious for cannibals.

As his boat drifted toward the island, the cannibals saw the boat. They grabbed their forks and napkins and ran out on the shore because they knew there was dinner, breakfast, supper, and brunches for a few weeks. They were praying to their gods, "Thank you, god, for this meal."

The ship captain, not a particularly religious man, realized his prayers probably were not going to be successful. So he went to Hudson Taylor, and he said, "Brother Taylor, you have to pray or we are about to be in heaven or hell. Pray for wind that will take this ship away from the natives who want to eat us."

Taylor said, "I will pray for wind if you will set the sails." The sails were down because there was no wind.

The Captain protested, "I can't do that. I will look like a fool if I pull up those sails with no wind."

Hudson Taylor said, "That is fine, but I will not pray until you do."

A little closer to the island, the captain said, "Set the sails. Set the sails."

Hudson Taylor went below and began to pray. You can imagine what happened a few moments later. Out of nowhere, the winds began to blow, and the ship sailed on to safety.

Was that a coincidence? Absolutely not. God heard a man's prayer. The man prayed in faith. He saw the wind before there was wind, and miraculously he lived.

MAKE A DECISION TO PRAY IN FAITH

I want to challenge you to pray in faith. Believe God loves you. Believe He cares, believe He listens, and believe He can and will do what you ask.

Christian, maybe that needs to be your commitment, "God, make me a person who prays in faith." Remember, praying in faith is more about what we believe about Him than it is about us. Make a commitment to trust God and to approach Him in faith as you pray from this point on.

God loves for you to pray in faith. It means you trust Him.
Believe He will do what you ask.
Tell us when He does. www.fbcruston.org

9

TO BE EFFECTIVE IN PRAYER, YOU MUST KEEP ON PRAYING

W illiam Carey is the father of the modern-day mission movement. He was an Englishman who felt the call from God to go and to be a missionary against much scorn and against much opposition, strangely, from the church leaders of his day. But he followed God's leading him to do that, and he laid a great foundation for foreign missions in his day and in the years to come.

A man who was writing his biography asked him, "To what, besides Jesus Christ, do you credit your success?" Carey thought for a moment, and he said, "I guess, after Jesus, I would simply say it's because I'm a plodder. I keep on keeping on. I put my hand to the plow, and I do not quit. If I owe my success to anything, it would be because I keep on keeping on."[1]

In life, much of success boils down to not quitting when we want to quit or to staying with something. Did you know in prayer that is true, too? I want us to look at persisting in prayer, praying and staying with prayer. This is such a great subject. I think we may have lost or may be on the verge of losing some great things because we are failing here. We need to look at this subject of persisting in prayer.

PRAYER IS A LIFETIME COMMITMENT

Prayer is a lifetime commitment. Prayer is a lifetime cause. It is not just a cause when you are in the youth group. It is not just a cause for college students. It is not just a cause for young adults. It is a cause for all of us until we go on to glory.

"Jesus told His disciples a parable to show them that they should always pray and not give up" (Luke 18:1). When Jesus taught them they should always pray and not give up, that means this is something that ought to be done. It is not just an option or a suggestion. This is something we ought to do.

When Luke says, "He taught them that they should always pray and not give up," it is the picture of Jesus saying, "It is by the very nature of things." By the very nature of spiritual things and of life, there is an unavoidable urgency that when it comes to prayer we don't quit. Prayer, by the very nature of what it is, is a lifetime commitment.

It is also interesting that the word for prayer in this passage is a word that is all-encompassing. It is a devotional, prayer-time word. God says we need to develop the habit of encompassing all aspects of prayer: praising God, forgiving others, confessing our sins, thanking God, praying for others, praying for ourselves, listening to God. We need to develop this lifetime habit of persisting in prayer.

Jewish people in Jesus' day set aside three specific times each day they were to pray: nine a.m., twelve noon, and three p.m. One Bible scholar said many Jewish people would not pray more than those three times a day because they did not want to pester God.

Let me tell you some good news: you cannot pester God enough. You can pester your husband or wife, your children or parents, your grandchildren or grandparents. We can pester each other enough, can't we? We can, be honest. We cannot pester God enough. Prayer needs to be something you and I can say, "It is a part of who we are the rest of our life."

Dr. Henry Blackaby, one of our great Southern Baptist leaders, said we should never look at prayer as just a one-shot affair. Never look at prayer as a one-shot affair. Prayer is a lifestyle commitment.

Dr. Henry Halley, a great Bible scholar in an earlier generation, said, "When it comes to prayer, to be effective in prayer takes a lifetime of study and severe discipline."[2] To really learn how to pray, Dr. Halley said you have to study it for the rest of your life. It takes severe discipline, and it takes persistence. If we want to be effective in prayer, realize it is a lifetime commitment.

Have you ever been told by a doctor or a boyfriend or girlfriend or husband or wife, "You need to diet and exercise?" I am told that regularly: "Diet and exercise." Now, for how long was this suggestion meant to be? Was it for a few months or a few years? No. Diet and exercise, to be effective, is a lifetime commitment. So it is with prayer. Prayer needs to be a lifetime commitment.

God said this: "Devote yourselves to prayer" (Col. 4:2). If you are devoted to a person, you are dedicated to them. You are sold-out and committed to them. If you are devoted to a certain college and to their athletic teams, that means you are sold-out to them, committed to them.

God says, "I want you to be dedicated to prayer, devoted to prayer. And I want it to be a lifestyle commitment." Jesus taught His disciples they should always pray and not give up. A very important principle about prayer is to stay with it.

WHY SHOULD WE PERSIST IN PRAYER?

Why is it necessary to persist in prayer? Let me give you a great reason. We should persist in prayer because God says we should.

Here is something about prayer that we need to embrace. If you try to figure it all out rationally, you never will. We cannot get our hand on God. He is not an engineering formula or a mathematical equation.

When Jesus says to persist in prayer, one reason we need to do it is simply because He says it. It may not make sense. It may not seem logical. You may have a hundred excuses otherwise. God says it; you do it. Let me give you some other reasons.

We Have Free and Sinful Natures

We need to persist in prayer because you and I have sinful, free natures, don't we? I have a sinful, free nature. By free nature, I mean God did not make me a robot. I need to persist in prayer in my own life because I can be right with God tonight and be off-base tomorrow. You can say that about me, but it is true about you, too, isn't it? One reason we need to persist in prayer is we have a sinful nature. We have a tendency to bend off and go the wrong way. We need to persist in prayer for ourselves because of that.

Other People Have a Free and Sinful Nature

Another reason we need to persist in prayer is for other people because they, too, have a free and sinful nature, don't they? They do. People you are praying for have the ability to do right or to do wrong. They have the ability to be on the right course tonight and be way off-course a month from now. We persist in praying for other people because they have a free nature and a sinful nature that can lead even the best of people down the wrong road. We need to persist in prayer for them.

We Live in a Sinful World

It is especially important for us to persist in prayer because we live in a sinful world that is never going to be perfect until Jesus comes and makes it right. We must persist in prayer because we live in a sinful world.

Jesus was talking about a corrupt judge.

> He told His disciples a parable to show them they should always pray and not give up. He said: "In a certain town there was a judge who neither feared God nor cared about men. And there was a widow in that town...."

A widow in that day was the picture of utter helplessness, totally dependent on other people. Jesus said the widow kept coming to the judge with a plea:

"Grant me justice against my adversary." For some time he refused, but finally, he said to himself, "Even though I don't fear God or care about man, yet because this widow keeps bothering me, I will see that she gets justice so that she won't eventually wear me out with her coming."

Luke 18:1-5

Jesus used this story to teach that we ought to keep praying, and that things happen when we do keep praying. One reason we ought to keep praying is we live in a sinful world.

SPIRITUAL WARFARE IS GOING ON

This next reason to persist in prayer is hard to explain, but it is so real. We live in a world where spiritual warfare is going on. We live in a world in the middle of spiritual warfare. There is God. There is a real devil. One of the most effective lies the devil can get us to believe is that he is not real. There is a real devil, there are real demons, and there is spiritual warfare that takes place in our midst. That is Bible, and that is truth. Jesus said, "You should always pray and not give up." One reason is because of the spiritual warfare.

Daniel prayed, and God sent an angel who said:

Do not be afraid, Daniel. Since the first day that you set your mind to gain understanding and to humble yourself before God, your words were heard, and I have come in response to them. But the prince of the Persian kingdom resisted me twenty-one days. Then Michael, one of the chief princes came to help me, because I was detained there with the king of Persia.

Daniel 10:12-13

That is peculiar, isn't it? Many Bible scholars believe that mention of the king of Persia is talking about a demon. Daniel prayed. God heard the request. God granted the request, but because of the spiritual battles going on it actually took three weeks for His answer to be delivered to Daniel.

Why should you continue to pray? The devil hates you. The devil hates your prayer life. Once you become a Christian, his goal is to destroy you. His goal is to fight your spiritual progress at every point, to rob you of your joy, and to ruin your life. He doesn't want you to pray. One reason we need to persist in prayer is because all of that is going on.

Persisting in Prayer Tests Us

One last reason to keep praying is persisting in prayer tests us. It tests us. Jesus says you should always pray and not give up. Have you ever wanted to quit in prayer? Isn't there a time you should just say, "It isn't going to happen; this person I am praying for is never going to get right," or "This situation is never going to get better"? One thing Jesus is trying to teach us is to stay in there.

Often in the New Testament, the words *test* and *tempt* are the same Greek word, and it depends on the context as to what the words are trying to imply.

Always remember this: Jesus never tempts us to do wrong. Satan does. Satan uses opposition to our prayers to tempt us to quit and to tempt us to throw in the towel. I believe God allows some of that to happen to test our commitment, to test our sincerity, and to test our obedience to Him in that area. One reason we have to persist in prayer is that it is a test of our character and our obedience to God. But let me tell you, we need to persist. We do.

ARE THERE EXCEPTIONS TO PERSISTING IN PRAYING?

Now, I am going to throw you a curve ball. Is there ever a time to stop praying about something? I have just told you prayer is a lifetime commitment. I have given you five reasons you should keep praying. Does there ever come a time you and I should stop praying about an issue?

NEVER QUIT PRAYING ABOUT OTHERS' SPIRITUAL NEEDS

When it comes to other people and their spiritual and character issues, should we ever quit praying. The answer is no. When you are praying for another person to be saved, to grow in their relationship with Jesus, or to have integrity in character; never, ever stop praying for them.

At the first church I pastored, I remember someone telling me a story about a lady who prayed more than twenty years for one of my men. After twenty years, this man became a Christian. Was she right to pray for that man that long? Absolutely! When it comes to praying for other people—their protection, their safety, their salvation, their relationship with God, their character—never, ever stop praying for them until one of you goes on to somewhere else, you, I hope, to heaven.

NEVER QUIT PRAYING ABOUT YOUR SPIRITUAL CONCERNS

When it comes to your own spiritual and character issues, don't ever quit praying. There should never be a day you and I stop saying, "God, help me to be more like you. God, help me to have more integrity. Help me to have more character. Help me to be more loving. Help me to be more kind. Help me to be more like you, Jesus." There should never, ever be a time we stop praying about that.

THERE ARE TIMES TO LET GO A PRAYER REQUEST

There may be a time in our praying we need to let things go. Let me give you a few examples. When Jesus was in the Garden of Gethsemane, He prayed three times, "God, I would rather go another route than be whipped and beaten and hung on a cross and murdered. Can we go another route? Nevertheless, God, what You want, may it be done" (Mark 14:32-39, *Author's paraphrase*). Three times He prayed. Then He let it go, and He obeyed, didn't He?

Paul prayed three times and said, "Jesus, remove this thorn from my flesh," but he received a clear answer from God, "It's not going to happen, Paul. It's there for a reason, and that's My Will. You can let it go and quit praying about it. Paul, accept it" (2 Cor. 12:7-9, *Author's paraphrase*).

When I was in college, I was dating a girl and we really liked each other. We prayed and said, "God, we want to be together forever." We thought we did. "God, let us date each other and marry each other." We prayed that a few months, and do you know what we kept hearing back from heaven? "No." We finally realized we were not meant for each other in the romantic realm. God said to us, "Okay, I wanted you to pray, and what you prayed was fine. Now hear me, and let it go. It's over."

A man I knew wanted a certain job. He prayed for that job. The job came open, but he did not get it. Several years later, the same thing happened. He had been praying for years about that same job.

Finally, it got to the point my counsel to him was: "You need to take some time and listen to God. You need to say, 'God, do You want me to have this job? If You do, I'll keep pushing in prayer. If You don't, God, tell me no, and I'll let it go.' " He came back later and told me, "God said that job is not for me."

This takes a lot of wisdom. This takes coming to the point where you are willing to say, "God, show me if Your answer is no." And when God says no, don't keep banging the doors to heaven. You let it go.

But let me remind you, with so many things we need to keep banging on those doors. Personal, spiritual, moral, and ethical matters—you never quit praying for them. You never quit praying for that person to be saved. You never quit praying for your own life. For your church, you never quit praying. For all those things, you never do.

WILL PERSISTING IN PRAYER PAY OFF?

Will it pay off if we persist in prayer? I'll be honest with you. I don't like to invest much time in something that doesn't work. I don't want to persist in prayer just for the fun of it. I want to know: Is it going to matter? Is it going to make a difference? And I want to tell you with a resounding "Yes," it will. For you and me to keep praying for weeks or days or years, yes, it will pay off.

Jesus taught his followers this parable to let them know it mattered. He said, "Here is a wicked, old, mean judge, but because the widow was persistent he will finally give in. And if a wicked, old judge responds to persistence, won't a loving God?" (Luke 18:1-5, *Author's paraphrase*).

Jesus told another story of a man who went to his friend at midnight, and he said:

> "Friend, lend me three loaves of bread because a friend of mine on a journey has come to me, and I have nothing to set before him."
>
> Then the one inside answers, "Don't bother me. The door is already locked, and my children are with me in bed. I can't give you anything.
>
> (Luke 11:5-7)

The story goes on that he keeps knocking and, finally, the man inside gets up and gives him what he wants so he will leave him alone.

GREAT THINGS HAPPEN WHEN YOU PERSIST IN PRAYER

Jesus told His disciples to teach people if you keep on persisting in prayer, great things will happen. Great things will happen. I don't understand why this works the way it does. I just accept it in faith.

You remember I told you that at my first church a lady had prayed twenty years for a man to be saved. After twenty years, He was saved. For twenty years she prayed for him, and for twenty years as an adult he came to church, but he was not interested in God. Twenty years later, he was saved.

I have already mentioned another man from a little church I served in for a while in Tennessee. He was a leader of the church where I was interim pastor before I moved to Texas to go to seminary. He told me a great story of a lady in that community whose husband was a bad character. He would take her to church and drop her off. Then he would go to the city square and sit and whittle until church was over, and he would come pick her up. For thirty-five years that went on, and for thirty-five years she begged God to convict and save her husband. After thirty-five years of prayer, he was saved.

Dr. R. A. Torrey was a great minister at the turn of the nineteenth and twentieth centuries. At one time he pastored a church in Minneapolis, Minnesota. Two ladies who did not know each other came to him separately, and each of them said, "Dr. Torrey, my husband is not a Christian. Will you pray for him to be saved?" He made a commitment in his heart and to the ladies that he would pray for those men regularly until he heard they became Christians or until they died or he died. Years went on, and he went to England. He returned to America as an evangelist.

One evening he was leading a crusade in Minneapolis, and two men were sitting together in the congregation. He didn't recognize them, and he found out later they didn't know each other. He gave the invitation, and both of those men were saved. As he talked to them, he found out they were the men that for twenty years he had been praying for. They had never met each other, but that night they were sitting side by side in the sanctuary.[3]

Was that a coincidence? No. Absolutely, it was not. That was an answer to persistence in prayer. That was saying, "God, I'm not going to quit. God, I'm going to keep on praying until I die, they die, or something happens." Isn't that great?

George Muller was a great Christian leader who ran an orphanage in Bristol, England. Muller was a young man when he became a Christian. Five of his best friends were not Christians. Muller wrote their names in the front of his Bible, and he said, "I'm going to pray for these men until they get saved or I die or they die."

He prayed for one year, two years, four years. Nothing happened. Would you have been discouraged? After five years, one of them was saved. He went on six, seven, eight, nine; nobody else was saved. Ten years later, the second friend was saved. He continued twenty years and still only two were saved. Twenty-five years later, the third man was saved. Thirty-five, forty, fifty years later, after fifty years, the fourth man was saved. After fifty-two years, Muller died. Only four of them were saved. Two months after Muller's death, the fifth man was saved.[4]

You know, all those men have died and are in heaven tonight. How many of them do you think wish Muller had quit praying for them? Is that not a wonderful story? Is that not an unbelievable story? I can't explain to you rationally how it works, but I know God says, "Keep praying, keep praying, keep praying." When you get discouraged, when you become disheartened, keep praying.

Persisting in Prayer Pays Off

Recently, I read a great story about a man who was a Methodist preacher in Texas for years. He told a story about himself when he turned twelve years old. He thought he was old enough to plow in the field. Now, this was when plowing was done with mules and horses, and he kept telling his daddy, "Daddy, I'm old enough to plow."

Finally, his daddy said "Okay, let's go do it." He said early in the morning about five o'clock they went out and hitched the mule to the plow, and they began to plow. He said about nine-thirty, it really wasn't fun anymore. He said around noon he was about dead, and he figured his father, who was kind and gentle, would say, "Son, go on and be a boy and go play the rest of the day." He didn't say that.

About two o'clock, he said, "Daddy, I've had enough plowing. I'm ready to go swimming."

His father said, "No, son, look at the sun." He said, "The sun's not down yet, son. As long as the sun is up, we keep on plowing. We are going to plow until the sun goes down."

What I want to tell you about prayer—you keep plowing until the sun goes down. You get discouraged, you get weary, you get heart-broken, you want to quit, you want to go do something else that's fun; you keep praying. You keep praying till the sun goes down. You keep praying till God takes you on to heaven or takes them to heaven. You keep praying till He comes back, and we don't have to pray anymore. But I challenge you, and encourage you, and plead with you to believe persisting in prayer pays off. Why? Believe it pays off because Jesus Christ said it does. Keep on plowing.

DECIDE TO PERSIST IN PRAYER

Christian, do you need a spiritual B_{12} shot? Do you need encouragement? Jesus says, "Keep on. Keep on praying."

Christian, maybe what you need to do is say, "God, I'm going to keep on. I'm going to keep on." Do you know what our churches need more than anything else? We need people who will keep praying for their church and won't quit, people who will keep on, keep on, keep on. Maybe that needs to be your commitment. Make a commitment to be a man or woman who really prays and who will never quit praying!

Are there prayers you've quit praying too soon?
Dust them off. Jesus asks us not to give up.
Keep on praying. www.fbcruston.org

10

A VERY IMPORTANT AND NEGLECTED PART OF PRAYER: LETTING GOD TALK TO US

A psychologist studied people and their personalities, and he developed what he thought was a way of looking at people's ears that would reveal what they were like. This is a true story.

He said he could look at people's ears and know what their personality was like. He said if you had large, rounded ears you had a strong nature, you were interested in truth and ideals, and you were ambitious. He found that people with small ears tended to have personalities that persevered. They were prudent and had will power. He determined that people with oval-shaped ears loved to study and were perfectionists.

If your right ear is bigger than your left, you lean toward living the fantasy life. If your left ear is bigger than your right, you tend to be a little more rational.

I want to tell you my spiritual thoughts on that. Who knows? And who cares? Ears probably were not meant to be a psychological evaluative tool. Ears were given so we could hear, and I want us to think about using our ears, not our physical ears but our spiritual ears, to listen to God.

LISTENING TO GOD

Did you know that part of praying should be listening? In Second Samuel, chapter five, we are going to be looking at an often neglected and misunderstood part of praying, and that is listening to God.

We have been considering the importance of developing a prayer life where we spend time daily praising God, getting our heart right with others, confessing our sins, thanking God, praying for others, and praying for ourselves. We have looked at praying in faith and persisting in prayer. Now, I want us to think about listening to God in prayer, not only talking but listening, as an aspect of prayer that needs to be included in our prayer life.

GOD SPEAKS THROUGH THE BIBLE

God speaks clearly through the Bible, doesn't He? You say, "I want God to speak to me." I want to tell you something you probably already know. God speaks clearly through the sixty-six-books-in-one called the Bible.

In David's day, God spoke clearly through the Bible, too. What Bible did David have? David had Genesis, Exodus, Leviticus, Numbers, Deuteronomy, and probably some more books of the Old Testament. That would have been his Bible. His Bible told him that God spoke through it. Joshua 1:8 says, "Don't let the Book of Law depart from you. You meditate on it, you think about it, you study it, and you live it out" (*Author's paraphrase*).

David's own words in Psalm 119:105 say about God's Word, and this certainly would have applied to his Bible, "It is a lamp to my feet and a light to my path." David had some of our Bible, which was God's perfect Word to him, That was his instruction. God's Word was clear to him when it spoke about how he should live.

Many times I hear people say, "I want God to speak to me." Often that is a code for "I need to see a flashing light. I need a dove to descend so I'll know what God is trying to tell me." More often than not, God is not going to speak in that way. One way God wants to speak to you and me, like He wanted to speak to David, is through the Bible.

When you want to know what God has to say, the first thing to do is to read your Bible. How can we be a church doing God's business if we don't know the Bible? How can you live the Christian life if you don't read your Bible? I have said it a hundred times and I'll say it a hundred more: every Christian ought to read the New Testament every year. Do that to know what God wants to say to you.

George Washington, our first President, said, "It is impossible to govern without the Bible." Amen to George. I wish our modern politicians would believe that today. I want to tell you this: it is impossible to live the Christian life without the Bible, without knowing it and learning it more and more.

WHEN THE BIBLE IS SILENT

God clearly speaks through the Bible. But here is a problem David ran into, and so do we. The Bible is silent on some issues in life. Every issue the Bible addressed to David and every issue the Bible addresses to you and me is God's Word on it. When the Bible says, "Do not commit adultery," you do not have to pray about that. When the Bible says, "Do not steal," don't sit in Wal-Mart praying, "Should I stick this in my coat? God, show me Your Will." God's Will is clear on that. When the Bible says it clearly, that is God's Word on it.

Much of our struggle in life comes when the Bible is not clear on issues. Some people would say, "Well, just do whatever you want to do." I believe that is absolutely wrong. I think God wants to give us guidance in every area of our life.

This is what happened with David. The Philistines heard David had been anointed king over Israel, so they went up in full force to search for him, not to congratulate him but to rough him up.

But David heard about it and went down to the stronghold. Now the Philistines had come and spread out in the Valley of Rephaim; so David inquired of the Lord, "Shall I go and attack the Philistines? Will You hand them over to me?"

And the Lord answered him, "Go, for I will surely hand the Philistines over to you." So David went and "there he defeated them." [David] said, "As waters break out, the Lord has broken out against my enemies before me. So that place was called Baal Perazim. The Philistines abandoned their idols there, and David and his men carried them off."

It happened again.

Once more, the Philistines came up and spread out in the Valley of Rephaim; so David inquired of the Lord, and he answered, "Do not go straight up, but circle around behind them and attack them in front of the balsam trees. As soon as you hear the sound of marching in the tops of the balsam trees, move quickly, because that will mean the Lord has gone out in front of you to strike the Philistine army."

2 Samuel 5:17-24

Verse twenty-five says David did exactly what God told him to do. Here is David's predicament. The Philistines were coming to kill David and his men. David's Bible did not address what he needed to do. David didn't just say, "I'm wise. I'm smart. I'm intelligent. I'm educated. I will move forward in the tradition of my fathers." He didn't say that. He said, "God, what in the world do I need to do?" He prayed, and then he listened to God, didn't he?

There are issues in your life, and in my life, and there will be plenty of issues in the life of our church for which the Bible will not give us clear direction. We can choose to operate in one of many ways. We can just say, "We'll take a vote, and the majority wins, and we'll say, "That is God's Will." The majority decision is not always God's Will. We know that from the Bible. We can say, "We've always done it this way, so we are going to always do it that way." We can say, "We need to do something new, so we are going to do this." Or we can say, "Let's seek God, and find out what God has to say about it." That's a neat concept, isn't it? It's a great concept.

How does this play out in your personal life? Let's say you are a single person, and you want to date and marry someone. God lays out some standards in the Bible that a Christian should date and marry a committed Christian, but that gives a lot of room for wiggle. Many people who are Christians would not make you a good husband or wife, correct? That is true, I promise you. And that is where you need to be praying and listening to the Holy Spirit and hearing Him say, "That is not the right person for you," or "This is the right person for you."

Some of you who are married may be offered another job or maybe two jobs, and they may be good jobs, not immoral jobs or dishonest jobs. Perhaps the pay is about the same and where you would be living is about the same. How should you decide which job to take? Some would say, "Just do what you want to do, and God will be pleased." I don't believe that. I think you need to pray and ask God to show you. You listen to God.

There are a lot of instances in life where the Bible will be clear on what to do. There are also many situations where the Bible does not give clear direction, and that is where praying and listening comes together. Have you heard someone say, "I'll pray about that and then let you know what I'm thinking"?

"Will you teach Sunday School?"

"I'll pray about it."

Most of us ministers think it's a no; it just has a delay to it.

But when you say, "I'll pray about it," what that is supposed to mean is this: "I don't know, and I am going to ask God, and I am going to let Him tell me," implying, whether it is ever done, that I will pray and I will listen for a response. I want us to see that as a vital part of prayer. Prayer is not only talking but it is listening to God, too.

How do we listen to God in prayer? It is easy for a preacher to tell you, "Go win the lost." It's easy to say, "Pray," and it's easy to say, "Listen in prayer." The hard thing is learning how to do some of these things. How do we do it?

PRESENT YOUR REQUESTS TO GOD

Here is a start. If you are facing decisions and you need to hear from God, present your request to God. Very simply, present your request or your problem to God.

In 2 Samuel 5:19, "David inquired of the Lord, 'Shall I go and attack the Philistines?' " Verse twenty-two says, "Once more the Philistines came up and spread out in the valley, so again David inquired of the Lord. 'What do I need to do?' " (*Author's paraphrase*)

This may sound really simple, but the first part of listening is telling God what is going on. You say, "God already knows." He does, but the Bible tells us God expects us and commands us to ask Him and to talk to Him. That is part of humbling us and teaching us to depend on Him.

When you are facing an issue, you pour it out to God. "God, here is the situation. I don't know what to do. I don't know whether I need to move, take that job, join this church, join that church, teach this class, not teach that class, sell the land, keep the land, give the million to the church or the two million. I'm struggling with which million to give." So you say, "God, show me." That sounds simple, but you do that. Lay it out to God. That is what David did.

BE QUIET AND LISTEN TO GOD

Once you have told God your problem, be quiet and listen. Oh, is this hard. Now, here is what we don't know. We do not know over how long a time these few verses took place. You and I read them in one minute. This could have been over an extended time period. I don't know. It certainly was not something David prayed about and two minutes later came back and said, "Okay, let's go fight them. Let's go and circle around the trees." David took time to be still and quiet and listen to God.

Psalm 46:10 is a great verse. It says, "Be still, and know that I am God." Would you agree that is extremely difficult in our society? It is very, very difficult for us in our society? Now, do you do this? This is how it works at my house. My wife and I really do communicate well, but a lot of times we talk while we are watching television and while we both are reading and petting a dog.

You do the same thing. You are brushing your teeth. You are combing your hair. You are talking to your kid, and you are talking to your spouse at the same time. And a lot of times, after it is repeated two or three times, you do get the message, don't you? That is how we communicate, unfortunately—with the radio on, while we are filling the car with gas, cleaning the window, and talking to two people at the same time.

It doesn't work that way with God. God said we need to be still and listen to Him. Ask God what to do, and then be willing to take the time to sit down and listen to Him.

In First Kings, Elijah needed to hear a word from God. His Bible did not have the word he needed. There was an earthquake, there was thunder, but then God spoke to him. How? Do you remember? God spoke in a still, small voice. A still, small voice is heard only when you take time to listen.

Bill Hybels, who pastors one of the largest and most effective churches in our country, is a man who is extremely busy. I heard Bill say in a lecture that one of the most important things he does is take time to be still and listen to God.

I want to encourage you to develop a pattern to follow during your prayer time. After you praise God and get your heart right with others, then be quiet and say, "God, you talk a while."

You try this and at first you are going to feel strange. It will pay off in the long run. Then pray some more, thank God, confess your sins, pray for others. At the end of your prayer time, be still, and be quiet, and try again to listen to God. If this is new to you, it will take time, but this can become a wonderful part of your regular prayer time.

Certainly, when you have special problems and situations, you need to set aside time not only to talk to God about them but to sit down and be quiet and listen to God. If you want to hear God talk, and God wants to talk to you, you have to be willing to be quiet.

Let me ask you a question, a really important one, because if you are not interested in this, nothing else will matter. *Do you want to hear from God?* Then you have to give it some time. Be still and quiet before Him.

LISTEN TO GOD EXPECTANTLY

Listen to God expectantly. Expect God to speak to you. In verse nineteen, "David inquired of the Lord, 'Shall I go and attack the Philistines?' " In verse twenty-three, "David inquired of the Lord." Do you believe David was just doing a religious ritual? Do you believe he really was expecting God to tell him what to do? He was. He was saying "God, here is my problem. Now, I am all ears—oval or round or whatever—speak to me, God, speak to me."

When you and I begin to learn to listen to God, we have to expect God to talk to us. Don't try this a time or two and say, "God didn't say anything, this doesn't work." It does work, but you have to get in the habit of listening with expectancy.

James says this, "If any of you lack wisdom, ask God" (1:5-6). He wants to speak to you. Expect God to speak to you. God does not play around with people who do not believe that He is real and that He listens. Expect Him to speak to you.

LISTEN TO GOD PATIENTLY

Listen patiently. God may speak to you in a very relevant and powerful way about something in your heart. God may not. You may have a major issue you begin to pray about and to listen to God about tonight, and by tomorrow you may have a clear answer. You may not have a clear answer for several weeks.

Don't go in to listening to God like you are paying a psychologist to give you answers and tell you what you need to do the next moment. A good psychologist wouldn't do that anyway. God doesn't play that way. You are not putting a quarter in a machine to get an immediate response.

Be willing to listen patiently. Again, we do not know how long this process was for David and how long he listened before he got his response. Remember, spiritual warfare is going on. The devil does not want you to hear what God has to say. He is going to distract you, discourage you, and send you mixed messages while you are trying to hear God. This takes time.

I thought this week about when I came to pastor First Baptist Ruston. The process of my dealing with the pulpit committee extended over about four months before we all came together. After about six weeks, I felt like God was telling me I needed to stay where I was, and I believed He was telling me that for some time. Then I was asked again, "Pray about it some more." I did that, and over another three or four weeks I believe God clearly showed me this is where I needed to be. It takes time. Sometimes the bigger the decisions you are dealing with, the more you have to listen with patience if you want to hear what God has to say.

LISTEN TO GOD WITH AN OPEN MIND AND HEART

Listen with an open mind and an open heart. Many times we go to God and say, "God, what do *you* want me to do on this," and we already know what *we* want to do.

If you've ever raised a teenager, you know this is true. My daughters did this from time to time. They would come in on a Saturday night, and say, "May we go out tonight?" They would have their purses and two friends with them, and as they were walking toward the door say, "May we go out tonight?" They were not asking for our thoughts on that; they were asking for affirmation. I did that to my parents. I do that to my wife. We do those things, don't we? We say, "I really want to know what you are thinking," but we don't mean it.

I used to teach a Sunday School class in Texas, and we had a lot of young adults. In our discussions, people would raise their hands and say, "May I say something?" I'd say, "Yes."

Sometimes, just to throw them off and to mess with their minds, they would say, "May I say something," and I would say, "No." They would keep on talking anyway. They did not want my answer. They were going to talk anyway. Of course, I wanted them to talk; it was just fun to watch.

"Preacher, may I say something?"

"No."

"Well, listen, let me give you my thoughts on this."

We do that to God, don't we? "God, they have asked me to teach this Sunday School class. I don't want to do it. God, what do you want me to do? God, I don't want to do it."

I cannot tell you how many times I have had people come to me and say, "God is leading me to do something," when I know God wasn't leading them to do that simply because their behavior was against the Scriptures, against God's Word.

This is something everybody struggles with, but if you really want to hear God, you have to get in *neutral*. Do you know what neutral is? If you have driven an old stick-shift car, a tractor, or a riding lawnmower—you find neutral. Neutral means you can go in any direction pretty easily, right? Front, back—you can move either way.

God wants your heart and my heart to be in neutral. As a church, when we make decisions, many times we have already decided before we ever pray. This is what we want to do. "Oh, I'll pray about it." But when our fists are doubled when we are praying, we probably do not have an open heart, do we?

As a church, we have to have an open heart when we pray about things. As an individual, when I am praying about something, I have to have an open heart. I have to be in neutral.

I believe with all my heart that if God had told David, "David, you better get out of there," he would have gone. He did in other places in Scripture. David was open to what God had to say. We won't hear God if we are not open to God. We'll blame God and say "God said this," when He didn't. Be open to God, and do what He tells you. Make a habit of listening to God, presenting your requests, and being quiet before Him. Listen with expectancy and with an open heart.

HOW DO WE KNOW IT IS GOD SPEAKING?

How do we know when God is speaking? This is crucial. How do we know God's voice is the voice communicating to us? When you begin to pray and listen to God, several voices will come into your head. One is the devil's voice. When Jesus was fasting and praying, Satan began to talk to Him (Matt. 4:1-11), and Satan will try to influence your decisions and mine.

David wanted to build a temple, and Nathan, one of God's greatest prophets, said "David, do whatever you want to do. God is with you" (2 Sam. 7:3, *Author's paraphrase*). That night, Nathan went home and God said, "Nathan, you did not tell him the right message." David got a wrong word from a great man of God. As you and I begin to seek God and to listen to Him, the devil and even very good people, well-intended, godly people may say things to us that are contrary to what God wants to say.

GOD WILL NEVER CONTRADICT SCRIPTURE

How do we know it is God's voice we are hearing? He will never go against Scripture. The Holy Spirit speaking to your heart and mine will never lead you against the Bible. That is absolutely irreplaceable. The Holy Spirit wrote the Bible, therefore, He will not contradict the Bible.

I heard Paul Cho, pastor of the largest church in the world, which is in Seoul, Korea, tell a sad but probably common story in a sermon. One of his church leaders came to him several years ago and said, "Dr. Cho, God is leading me to divorce my wife and marry another woman. She and I both have prayed about it, and God is leading us to do this."

Dr. Cho said, "God is not leading you to do that. The Bible says for you to leave your spouse to marry someone else is never God's Will. It is against the Bible."

The man said, "No, God is leading us to do it." They did it, and it was devastating for everyone involved.

Please, know your Bible well enough to know God is never going to lead you to commit adultery, to commit sexual sin, to steal, lie, and cheat, or to gossip, or to be mean, or to be divisive. God never leads us against His Word. That is so, so important.

Someone asked, "How can you tell if a stick is crooked?" One of the best ways is to put it beside a stick that is straight. How can you tell if what you are hearing is from God? Make sure it doesn't go against the Bible.

GOD'S VOICE WILL BE CONSISTENT

God's voice will be consistent. Over time, God's voice will be consistent. Years ago, I heard a minister say that as he would pray about something, many times during the first few days he would go back and forth wondering if he were making the right decision, but over time he found the voice of God to be consistent.

I have found that in my own life. Sometimes during the first three or four days of praying about something I would be completely confused. I would say, "Yes, I am. No, I'm not. Yes, I am. No, I'm not." But over time God's voice would be consistent. Eventually, I would have uneasiness or peace from God that was consistent.

GOD MAY SPEAK THROUGH HIS PEACE

God often speaks in our hearts by giving us a sense of peace or uneasiness about what we need to do. In verse nineteen, "David inquired of the Lord, 'Shall I go and attack the Philistines?' " How did God respond to him? Did God write it in the clouds? I don't think so. Did God audibly tell David what to do? I really don't think so. I think He spoke to him in his heart just like He does us. Colossians 3:15 says, "Let the peace of God rule in your heart."

Charles Stanley said it so well. He said God doesn't have to speak in your ear, even though He can, because He lives in your heart. The Holy Spirit lives in your heart if you are a believer, and what will happen over time is that as you and I pray about things, "God, should I do this or do that?" often there will be real uneasiness or real peace about something. I have heard people say, "God has given me a freedom to do this," or "He has not given me a freedom." That is saying the same thing. I believe that is the voice of the Holy Spirit.

I want to tell you three ways to test the voice you are hearing:

1. Make sure it does not go against the Bible.
2. Make sure it is consistent over time.
3. Look for peace or uneasiness in your heart.

If you are praying with an open heart about doing something, and you have an uneasiness about it, do not move forward. Wait for the peace or uneasiness of the Holy Spirit to confirm it in your heart.

Let God Guide You in Making Decisions

Let me tell you some things I do. If I am facing a major decision, I get a piece of paper and I write Yes, No, or Uncertain at the top of that paper. I put down the dates and try to spend five to seven minutes a day just being quiet and saying, "God, what do you want me to do?" and I will write down my impressions. I may check four yeses and three noes. What is so neat is after a couple of weeks it begins to come together. There may be forty yeses and seven noes. I believe that is the Lord telling me I need to move forward with that.

When you face major decisions, I encourage you to do that. I encourage you to do that throughout your prayer time. Day in and day out, open your heart to God. Keep a pen and paper in hand, and listen to things God may tell you—people to call or to write or to go see. Listen to God.

Obey What God Tells You

Now, here is the thing that brings it all together. Obey what God tells you to do. David said, "What shall I do?" God said for him to go and attack them. What did David do? He went, and he attacked them. David inquired of the Lord. God said, "Do not go straight up but circle around behind them and attack them in front of the balsam trees." David did as the Lord commanded him.

Here is what is great. David did not know what to do. He asked God. God wanted to tell him what to do. David spoke to Him. God spoke to David. They spoke to each other, and David obeyed God.

Have you have ever been guilty of this? You say, "God, show me what to do." God tells you, and you don't do it. Have you ever been guilty of that? Nothing else matters at that point. You see, what we have to do is not only hear God but obey God.

I heard a cute story of a three-year-old little girl named Beverly. She was in the den at her Grandmother's house, and her Grandmother kept calling her, "Beverly, come in here now. It's time for supper." After about five minutes, the grandmother went in and said, "Beverly, did you hear me?" She said, "Grandmomma, my ears heard you, but my legs didn't." Be careful your ears hear God and your legs hear God. Obey what God tells you to do.

LISTENING TO GOD WILL CHANGE YOUR LIFE

In 1958, one of the famous Yogas made the statement that he believed if everyone in the world would practice transcendental meditation for twenty minutes twice a day, morning and evening, it would bring about a spiritual regeneration of the world. Well, obviously, since 1958, that has not happened, correct? I don't think twenty minutes twice a day of transcendental meditation will change the world.

Let me tell you something that will change you and me and change our church. Take time every day to meditate and listen to God. Listen to God about those major things you are facing. Listen to other people, but ultimately listen to God and say, "God speak to me." Listen to God and obey Him. It will change your life and my life if we will do that.

As a church, if we will do that, it will keep our church not only on the right track, it will keep us on a great track. Do you want to change your world? Do you want to change your life? Make listening to God a habit and a pattern of who you are.

I want to ask you, Christian, do you do this? Do you listen to God? Maybe you have been listening to God and you know what God is telling you, and it is time to obey Him. I want to challenge you to do that.

Christian, maybe you need to make a commitment to God and to yourself that you are going to begin to do this. Make listening to God a habit of your life. I challenge you to do that. I promise you it will change your life for the better if you will consistently listen to and obey God!

Will you let God talk to you?
Will you listen and respond to Him with obedience?
See how we seek to do that at www.fbcruston.org

11

ARE YOU REALLY CONNECTING WITH GOD WHEN YOU PRAY

On June 15, 1993, at ten-thirty in the evening, Ruth Nolen, a missionary in Argentina, had a strong sensation, a strong pull on her heart that she was to begin to pray for her fellow missionaries and friends Ed and Linda Ables. She did not know what was going on in their lives; they lived a couple of hundred miles away. But she really felt strongly burdened that she needed to pray for them. She prayed very hard for their safety and their protection and for God to bless them.

After she felt a sense of release from that, she began to try to get in touch with them by phone. What she found out was pretty eerie. At exactly ten-thirty, when Ruth had felt the strong pull of God to pray for Ed and Linda, they were being held up in what we call a home invasion. Some crooks had burst into their house and were robbing them and roughing them up. One of the criminals put a gun to Ed's head and pulled the trigger but nothing happened. They figured there were not any bullets in the gun and the crooks were just trying to intimidate him. What they found out when the police got the men and the gun was that there were bullets in the gun; it had just misfired.

Ed and Linda Ables survived that horrible ordeal. When they discovered Ruth had been impressed to pray for them at that exact time, they realized that the gun's misfiring was not a coincidence. It was God answering Ruth Nolen's prayer on their behalf. She connected with God powerfully in prayer, didn't she? [1]

A RELATIONSHIP WITH JESUS CHRIST IS KEY TO CONNECTING WITH GOD IN PRAYER

When you pray, do you want to connect with God? People who are interested in God want to connect with Him in prayer. Jesus talked about connecting in prayer, "If you remain in me and my words remain in you, ask whatever you wish, and it will be given you" (John 15:7). The first principle for an effective prayer life is this: *The key to connecting with God in prayer is your relationship with Jesus Christ.* But let me tell you, there are people who will debate that point.

Several years ago, a survey was done in America. People were asked: "If you pray, who do you think you are talking to?" Or when a Christian prays or when a Muslim prays or a Hindu or a Buddhist or when anybody just talks to the Great Spirit; what is going on? The vast majority of American people said it is all going to the same place. They said it does not matter about your religion or whether you believe in Jesus, that it is all going to go to God.

I want to tell you from the Bible we cannot accept that as being true. Jesus Christ made some exclusive claims about Himself that have a profound effect on everything—heaven and hell, eternity, life here, and prayer, too. Jesus Christ said, "I am the way, and the truth, and the life. No man comes to the Father except through me." (John 14:6). When it came to heaven, when it came to a relationship with God, Jesus was narrow-minded, wasn't He? He was. Those are not just the words of a pastor or priest. Those are the words of Jesus.

Some of Jesus' disciples said later, "Salvation is found in no one else, for there is no other name under heaven given to men by which we must be saved" (Acts 4:12). These men were followers of Christ. They were speaking to the Jewish leaders of the day, and they told them, "There is only one way to go to heaven, and that is through Jesus Christ."

The Bible is clear, even though society is repulsed by this today. The Bible says the only way to heaven is through Jesus Christ. The only way to have a relationship with God the Father is through Jesus Christ.

ABIDE IN CHRIST

Your relationship with Jesus has a profound effect on your prayer life. We have Jesus' words, "If you remain in me and my words remain in you, ask whatever you wish, and it will be given you" (John 15:7). Jesus was claiming this: not only is salvation through Him but that the only way we can come to know God the Father is through Jesus Christ. We will be in heaven someday only if we have a relationship with Jesus Christ.

The key to connecting with God in prayer is our relationship with Jesus Christ. Depending on your Bible translation, you may read "If you remain in me" or "If you abide in me." Abiding and remaining in Christ are the keys to connecting with God in prayer. Jesus said if you do this, you can ask and you are going to see the Father answer in great ways. Ask and great things will happen.

Now what does it mean to *abide in Christ*? What does it mean to *remain in Christ*? If this is the key to connecting with God in prayer, we need to know what it means. Let me give you several thoughts.

Abiding in Christ means You Are a Christian

Abiding in Christ means you are a Christian. Jesus said, "If you remain in me and my words remain in you, ask whatever you wish, and it will be given you." That word *remain* or *abide* means *to dwell in* something or *to be conformed to* something. It literally means to be *in* something. You are not *in* Jesus Christ until you are a Christian. Prayer, a real prayer life beyond the call to ask Jesus to be our Lord and Savior, begins when we become a Christian.

When I was in high school, I was not a Christian but I prayed in emergency situations. "The parents are going to find out." "The police are coming." I can remember before every football game in high school I used to pray two things, "God, may we win, and may

I score four touchdowns." We won a lot, but I never scored four touchdowns in a game.

Let me tell you why that was foolish praying. I didn't care about God three hours before that ballgame. I didn't care about God one minute after that ballgame. God was Santa Claus to me. "God, You are not going to run my life. God, I am not going to be surrendered to You. But, by the way, I would like You to bless my efforts tonight." I think God just smiled and said, "Not right now, son. We have a major issue called, 'you are not giving Me your life at this point.' "

You see, if we want to connect with God in prayer, it begins with having a relationship with Jesus Christ. Psalm 66:18, a very important verse, says: "If I had cherished sin in my heart, the Lord would not have listened." When there is sin in my life that has not been dealt with, I do not need to go to God and ask Him to bless my life and help me here and there. First, I need to deal with that sin.

The lost person has not dealt with that major obstacle called the *sin of unbelief.* The first step to connecting with God in prayer, as simple or as strange as it might sound, is that you have to have a relationship with Jesus Christ.

ABIDING IN CHRIST MEANS BEING RIGHT WITH OTHERS

Assuming you are a Christian, you have to make sure your heart is right toward other people. Jesus said, "If you remain in Me, if you dwell in Me, if you are being conformed to Me, if you are staying close to Me and My words remain in you. In other words, if you are living out in your life what I have taught through Scripture, then you can connect with God in prayer" (John 15:7, *Author's paraphrase*).

If you are a Christian, you have an opportunity to connect with God in prayer. But if you are bitter toward people, unforgiving toward people, or full of resentment; you are bouncing your words off the ceiling.

Jesus was talking to Christians during the Sermon on the Mount. He told them, "This is Christian forgiveness. "If you want me to forgive you, you forgive others. When you forgive others, I will forgive you. If you do not forgive others; I am not going to forgive you" (Matt. 6:14-15, *Author's paraphrase*).

Jesus was not talking about salvation. He was telling Christians how to live. And what Jesus said plainly is that if I walk around saying, "Praise God, hallelujah, I love Jesus," but in my heart I hate you—God has His arms folded when I am praying. God wants my relationship with other people to be right before He wants to start answering my requests. That is extremely important.

ABIDING IN CHRIST MEANS LIVING FOR JESUS

As a Christian, I have to be right with God. John 15:7 begins with a key word, *if.* "If you remain in Me, if you are close to Me, if you are dwelling in Me and My words remain in you, if you are living out what I have taught in Scripture and it is directing your life, *then* you pray and I will respond" (*Author's paraphrase*).

Jesus was talking about branches and vines but not the kind of branches and vines we have here. In the Holy Land where Jesus lived, vines spread all over the ground. The particular type of branch and vine Jesus was talking about needed meticulous care to keep it alive and fruitful. The ground around it had to be well tended, and the plant itself required radical pruning.

Jesus used that illustration to talk to Christians. He said, "If you want to connect with God when you pray, you have to give careful attention to your Christian life. You have to take living for Me seriously. You have to be meticulous in how you live out the Christian faith" (*Author's paraphrase*).

A friend of mine shared a story with me about one of his relatives that illustrates this very sadly. He said he believed the man was a Christian who was just away from God, and through the years he hardly ever went to church. He did not have an interest in the things of God and the Bible anymore. He didn't give. He didn't serve. But he had a particular need come up in his life.

He told my friend, "I go home every night and spend hours praying that God will give me what I want on this issue." My friend finally said to him, "To you, God is Santa Claus. You live as you want and do as you want with no regards to Him, but you think He is supposed to just give to you when you ask Him." God does not work that way. God says, "*If* you remain in me and my words remain in you, ask whatever you wish, and it will be given."

One way we can think about this is to suppose a couple of friends argue. The one who is wrong will not admit it and refuses his friend's attempts to make amends, but one day he asks the friend he has wronged to lend him some money.

"May I have a thousand dollars? Please, let me borrow a thousand dollars."

Now, even if his friend were able to do that, my guess is he will want to sit down and say, "Don't you think we ought to get some things right, first? Don't you think before you ask for something we need to restore our relationship?"

Let me tell you that is how God operates, not because He is trying to be mean but because He loves us. God says the key to our prayer life, one of the fundamental keys as a Christian, is we have to make sure we are doing our best to live for Him.

ABIDING IN CHRIST REQUIRES PRAYING PROPERLY

Another thought on connecting with God is that He requires us to pray properly, to pray sincerely. We pray in faith believing God will hear and answer our prayer. We pray consistently. We don't quit; we don't give up, and we make sure these other things are in line.

RIGHTEOUS PEOPLE CONNECT WITH GOD IN PRAYER

Jesus taught that if you are a Christian seeking to keep your life right with other people, if you are really trying to live for Him, and you are praying; you can connect powerfully with Him in prayer. If you do these things, you may "ask whatever you wish, and it will be given you" (John 15:7). Those words of Jesus are tremendously powerful.

James says the prayer of a righteous man is powerful and effective (5:16). When a righteous man prays—that is the key, a *righteous* man—when a person is right with Jesus Christ and trying to live for Christ, his prayer is powerful and effective. Not just any prayer, but the prayer of a righteous person reaches God.

126

Dr. Larry Dossey, a medical doctor, did his internship and residency at the V.A. and Parkland hospitals in Dallas, Texas. During this time he had an experience with prayer that deeply influenced his thinking about it.

As a young resident, he had a patient with cancer in both lungs. No effective treatment was then available. He explained the situation to his patient, who decided he wanted only to go home to die in peace. Dr. Dossey focused on managing his pain and keeping him comfortable. He noticed, however, that during visiting hours the man was surrounded continually by people from his church who had come to pray for him. Day after day this continued until he finally discharged the man to go home as he had requested.

About a year later, at the same hospital, Dossey got a call from a physician colleague of his. "Your old patient is back in the hospital with a bad case of the flu," the doctor told Dossey. "You should come by and see him. He wants to talk to you!"

Dossey was shocked that the man was still alive. When he had discharged him a year earlier, he assumed he'd be dead within a few days. The only "treatment" he'd had for his lung cancer had been prayer.

Dossey immediately went to the radiology department to look at the man's current chest x-ray and compare it with the one taken a year ago. The older x-ray showed cancer throughout both lungs, as Dossey remembered. The current chest x-ray was completely normal. Dossey was speechless. The man had had no medical therapy; his only "treatment" had been prayer. Dossey realized he had witnessed a miracle.[2]

I want to tell you that I have seen godly people pray for people, and I have seen the people they prayed for die. God does not say everyone will be healed. He absolutely does not. In fact, the Bible says everyone is going to die. That is Scriptural and certainly true. But great miracles happen because people connect with God when they pray.

I love the cartoon, *Family Circus*. One time it showed one of the little boys going to the mother and saying, "Momma, when we pray, does God have call screeners?"

Are there people screening our prayers? Let me tell you something, if you are a righteous man or a righteous woman, God does not have call screeners. When you pray, you connect with God Almighty. You connect powerfully with God Almighty. Everybody does not, but if you are a righteous teenager or a righteous senior adult, when you pray, you can connect with God powerfully. Tennyson said it so well, "More things are wrought by prayer than this world ever dreamed of."

Now I want to ask you a question, a very important and maybe a hard question. Are you connecting with God when you pray? When you pray, do things happen? When you connect with God, are there results where you can say, "I see God work as I pray"?

Several years ago the National and International Religious Service did a survey in America. They asked people, "What is your view on prayer?" About eighty-five percent of them said, "We believe God can hear, and we believe He could do something."[3] I want to tell you regardless of any survey, God can hear and God can act.

God is not on trial when I pray as to whether He can hear me and do something. I am on trial. You are on trial. Whether we connect with God is not a question of whether God is able. It is whether we are right enough with Him for Him to want to respond.

NOT CONNECTING WITH GOD IN PRAYER IS A PROBLEM

If we are not connecting with God when we pray, there is a problem. Jesus said if we remain in Him and His words remain in us, we may ask whatever we wish, and it will be given to us. If that is not happening for you, it could be you just are not praying. Let me tell you two other reasons you may not be connecting with God like you should.

CHRISTIANS AWAY FROM GOD ARE INEFFECTIVE

One reason Christians cannot connect with God in prayer is they may be away from God. Jesus says, "If you are remaining in Me, if you are abiding, if you are close to Me, if you are dwelling in Me, if My words are changing your life; you are going to pray. Not every answer will be yes. Some answers will be no; some will be wait. But you will see God work through your prayers."

Sometimes you may not see God do this because as a Christian you are not where you should be with Him. We are weak and ineffective on our knees when we are not where we should be with God.

In 1977, I worked in a gas station. One afternoon a man came in that station. He had on a sleeveless shirt, and I could not help but notice one of his arms was limp. I asked one of the men working with me about this man. He said the man a few years earlier had been in a terrible accident in a saw mill, and right at the shoulder his arm had been completely cut off.

They had taken the man to the hospital and were able to re-attach his arm. So when he walked in, it looked like he had two normal arms, but the arm that had been severed was not functioning. It was an arm, but it was weak and ineffective.

Some of us as Christians are like that when it comes to prayer. We are saved, and we look okay. We can pray, in public especially, and sound genuine, but really we are lifeless. We are weak, and we are ineffective. Someone coined this sad phrase: "Careless Christian living leads to powerless Christian praying."

God addressed some believers in these verses, "Is my arm too short to help you? Is my ear too dull to hear?" "No," God said. "It is your sins that have separated you from me" (Isa. 59:1-2). When I am doing only what I want; I need to understand I am laying my prayer life aside. Maybe the reason we are not connecting with God in prayer is we are Christians who are away from Christ.

ONLY CHRISTIANS CONNECT WITH GOD IN PRAYER

Another reason you may not be connecting with God when you pray is maybe you really are not a Christian. Jesus specified those who remain *in* Me. That is implying you belong to Him. Remaining means you are continuing to stay *in* Him, that you are a Christian.

The ones who remain in Jesus are going to pray, and things will happen. One reason some people do not seem to have success with prayer is they really do not know Jesus.

In 1998, a family joined my church one Sunday night, and I do not think I saw them again for several months. Easter Sunday the next year, the woman came to church by herself. She and her husband had divorced. When we gave the invitation, she came to the front, and she became a Christian that morning.

Her story was similar probably to many people you may know. She had made a decision earlier in her life she really did not mean or did not understand. But on that Easter morning she came, and she was saved.

I remember talking with her a few months later, and she said the neatest thing. She said, "I used to pray. I didn't pray a lot, but when I prayed I never felt like much happened. I didn't feel like I was connecting with God. It was weak and ineffective. But now when I pray I connect with God, and I see God work in my prayers."

I told her, you may not understand this theologically, but you do understand from experience that you have to belong to Christ to have a prayer life. She was right on target.

St. Augustine, an early Christian leader, made a strong statement. He said the reason many people in the church pray and nothing happens is they belong to the church, but they do not belong to Christ. One reason we may be ineffective in our prayer life is we really do not belong to Jesus.

CHRISTIANS NEED TO CONNECT WITH GOD

There is unlimited help and blessing in being connected with God. You and I need to connect with Him when we pray.

YOU NEED TO CONNECT WITH GOD FOR YOURSELF

I need to connect with God, and you need to connect with Him *for you*. Do you know that? That is not being selfish. When you pray, you need to be able to connect with God in your prayers for you.

You may say, "I am educated, and I am wealthy, and I am in great health. I don't need anybody, or I don't need God." You may not say that out loud. You may think that. You know, if you have the right kind of problem or pain in your life you will be screaming to

God, won't you? I need to connect with God for me. You need to connect for you.

YOU NEED TO CONNECT WITH GOD FOR OTHER PEOPLE

You need to connect with God for other people. There are people that need your prayers. They desperately may need your prayers within twenty-four hours. You and I need to be able to pray and make contact with God for other people.

I was in a revival service twenty years ago as a participant, not a leader. The preacher was an evangelist from East Tennessee named Henry Lingenfelter. He was a great and powerful preacher, and I remember one night he said something I will carry with me to my grave. He said:

> There are folks sitting out here tonight who may get a call later this week that someone you know and love desperately needs your prayers, and you are not going to be able to help them because your relationship to Christ is either nonexistent or so mixed up you are not going to get past the ceiling.

You know what, Henry was right on target.

ASK GOD TO HELP YOU CONNECT WITH HIM IN PRAYER

Remember that Billy Graham said he believes when we get to heaven God is going to show us a room with all the answered prayers we could have had if we had just asked. I believe that may be true. I believe there are a lot of things God wants to do for you and me; we just have not asked Him. But I believe there may be another room, too, a room God may show us of answers to prayers He could not give us because we were not right enough with Him for Him to give them.

DECIDE TO REMAIN IN CHRIST

Are you connecting with God as you pray? Maybe you are a Christian, and you are right with Jesus, and trying to live for Him.

Keep it up, good friend. This abiding, this remaining in Christ is a daily thing. Don't let it slip from you. Stay with it.

Remaining in Christ calls for a conscious choice, Christian, and you may need to come back to God so you can be effective in prayer. Why don't you make a fresh recommitment of your life to Jesus so you will be right with Him and so you can connect powerfully with Him in prayer?

Maybe you have realized your prayers are not being answered because you do not really have a relationship with God through Jesus Christ. I want to encourage you to ask Jesus to come into your heart to be your Lord and Savior. Surrender your life to Him now so you can find the life you truly need and want and so you can enjoy the privilege of true prayer. Do it today!

Are you right with God? Does He hear you pray?
These are the most important questions you'll ever ask.
Find help for your answers at www.fbcruston.org

12

SOME QUESTIONS COMMONLY ASKED ABOUT PRAYER

H ave you ever heard someone say, "The only dumb question is the one you don't ask?" I don't believe that. If you have heard some dumb questions, then you know that is not true. You *can* ask some dumb questions. But a lot of times it is dumb not to ask, and I want us to try to answer some very common and very good questions about prayer as we close out our study on prayer. It has been a joy for me. It's such a wonderful subject.

I want us to answer three common questions about prayer that are very important, and here is question number one.

WHAT IS PRAYING IN JESUS' NAME?

When we pray in the Name of Jesus Christ, what does that really mean? What is the significance of that?

In April 1994, I was pastoring near College Station, Texas. A lady came into my church who had not been in church very much, and she heard these Baptist people saying, "In the Name of Jesus, we pray, Amen."

She asked me, "What does it mean to pray in the Name of Jesus?" I was surprised because I had heard that expression all my life. You are just supposed to do that, aren't you? I thought: that is a great question.

WE ARE TOLD TO PRAY IN JESUS' NAME

Why do we pray in Jesus' Name? There are several reasons we pray in the Name of Jesus. One is we are told to. That is a pretty good reason when it is God who says it.

Jesus said, "I will do whatever you ask in my name so that the Son may bring glory to the Father. You may ask me for anything in my name, and I will do it" (John 14:13-14). Jesus added, "In that day you will no longer ask me anything. I tell you the truth, my Father will give you whatever you ask in my name. Until now you have not asked for anything in my name. Ask and you will receive, and your joy will be made complete" (John 16:23-24).

Now what Jesus has said is, "When you pray, when you approach the Father, approach Him in the Name of Jesus Christ, His Son, and when you pray and you come to Me, approach Me in My Name."

"Jesus, it is in your Name I am coming to You."

"God, it is in the Name of Jesus I come to You."

One reason we pray in the Name of Jesus Christ is God said to. Jesus said to. Now that is one good reason, but there is more to it than just that. Jesus never asked us to do something because He needed some extra verses in the Bible to complete the book of John. He always has a purpose, and it has a meaning.

PRAYING IN JESUS' NAME INVOLVES RELATIONSHIP

Praying in the Name of Jesus is not a magic formula. Jesus says, "You may ask me for anything in my name, and I will do it." (John 14:14). These are not mystical or magical words that say you can live as you want, do as you want, and then say, "Jesus, I want to win the lottery, and in Your Name I pray, Amen."

"Jesus, bless our business meeting, but we already have plans to do wrong. Amen, in Your Name." It doesn't work that way. Praying in Jesus' Name is not a magic formula.

Praying in Jesus' Name is what we do not only because Jesus said to but because it involves our relationship with Him. He says, "Ask me for anything in my name, and I will do it."

A man talking with me about prayer quoted John 14:14 to me and said, "You go and you pray in Jesus' Name, and He is going to do it."

I said, "Look at verse fifteen in your Bible. 'If you love me, you will obey what I command.' " When you tie John 14:14 in with the verse that follows, you will see it is talking about having a relationship with Jesus Christ.

"Some trust in chariots, and some in horses, but we trust in the name of the Lord our God" (Ps. 20:7). The Old Testament was written in Hebrew. Jesus grew up in a Jewish family, a Hebrew family, and to them the idea of a *name* did not mean just a title; it was talking about the whole person, who they were. The psalm writer is not saying we just trust in the *word* God; He is saying we trust in the *person* who is God. To the Hebrew, trusting in God's Name meant they were trusting in God.

Praying in the Name of Jesus is not implying a magic formula; it is implying you and I have a relationship with Jesus Christ. It is saying, "Jesus, I belong to You. I belong to You, therefore, I belong to God the Father. God the Father, I belong to You because I belong to Jesus Christ." It is implying that I am a Christian who is living for Jesus and walking with Jesus. It is implying I know Him intimately. Praying in the Name of Jesus is not about using a magic formula; it is about having an intimate relationship with God through Jesus Christ.

GOD LOVES THE NAME OF JESUS

I get phone calls every now and then at home just like you do at eight o'clock at night when you do not want a phone call. And when they say, "Is this Robert?" or when they call the church and say, "Is this the pastor, Pastor Craig?" I know, I know, I know, it is somebody selling something. Nobody that knows me calls me Pastor Craig.

Nobody who knows me calls me Robert.

"Robert, how are you doing, Brother?"

"Well, I was doing great until you called me. I don't want it, whatever it is. Giving away a million dollars? I don't want it tonight. Call my wife."

But when someone calls me, and they want to talk to Chris, that probably means they know me a lot better than that one that wants to talk to the pastor or the one who wants to talk to Robert.

Let me tell you a little story about my father. My father's name was Robert E. Craig. Interestingly enough, the "E" stood for nothing. The "E" stood for E. I think my grandfather, before he was a Christian, had been hitting the Arkansas moonshine when they named my father just "E"—Robert E Craig. And growing up, they didn't call him Robert, they called him Jack. My Father was a college administrator, and through the years most of the people I was around growing up called him Dr. Craig.

Occasionally, I would meet someone, and they would say, "I know Robert. I know Robert Craig." I thought: you don't really know him. Nobody who knows him calls him Robert. And somebody who was really trying to butter me up would say, "I know old Bob Craig." Nobody called my father Bob. If you said to me you knew Bob Craig that meant you didn't know my father.

But I want to tell you, to this very day, if somebody came to me and said, "I knew Jack Craig," that would get my attention. That is what my momma called him. That is what his momma called him. That is what his brothers and sisters called him. The people that knew him personally called him Jack, and if somebody called me or saw me and said, "I knew Jack Craig," I would pay attention to them because I loved him. And if they called him that, that would mean they knew him, and I would be really interested in helping them or paying attention to what they had to say.

You know what, when you go to God and you mention the name Jesus, He becomes really interested because there is no more precious name in the world to Him than that. When we approach the Father in the Name of Jesus, we are approaching Him in a name that gets His attention. We are approaching Him in the Name of the One He loves the most, His Son.

There is a beautiful song, "There is Power in the Name of the Lord."[1] There is power in the Name of the Lord when you know the Lord. We pray in the Name of Jesus because we are told to. We pray in the Name of Jesus because we know Jesus, because we are intimate with Him, because when we approach God the Father in the Name of Jesus we are approaching Him in a name He loves, and

He will listen to what we want to talk about with Him. I hope you understand that is why we pray in the Name of Jesus.

DOES GOD ALWAYS ANSWER OUR PRAYERS?

Another important question I want to answer is: does God always answer our prayers? How many times have we heard someone say, "I pray and nothing seems to happen?" Does God always answer our prayers?

GOD DOES NOT ALWAYS ANSWER PRAYER

I am going to shock you, I think, with this. God does not always answer prayer. No, He doesn't. Sometimes God absolutely does not answer our prayers. If you are not a Christian, you need to come into a relationship with God. He wants your life before He grants your requests. In Psalm 66:18 applies to a Christian or a non-Christian when it says if I have regarded or kept sin in my heart, the Lord will not hear me. Christian, I want to tell you, you and I cannot live as we want and go to God in prayer and expect Him to respond.

Jesus said, "If you forgive others, I will forgive you. You don't forgive them, I won't forgive you" (Matt. 6:14). I want to tell you that if you want to hold on to bitterness and an unforgiving spirit, that is your choice. God lets you, but check your prayers off because they are not going to affect anything.

I want to mention again something I heard Bill Hybels say. "Why in the world do you think if you don't honor God's request, He would honor yours?" Isn't that good? "I don't have to do what God wants me to do, but He'd better listen and follow me." That is so backwards. Why would God honor our request when we are not honoring His?

The simple fact is there are times God will not honor your prayers or mine. You have heard the term *bouncing prayers off the ceiling*. That happens everyday. If you are not a Christian, you need to come into a relationship with Jesus. If you are a Christian, you'd better take seriously keeping your life right and in line with God. Prayer is about relationship with Jesus. If we are not right there, God does not answer our prayers.

GOD ALWAYS ANSWERS CERTAIN PRAYERS

Here is some great news. If you are a Christian trying to live in a right relationship with God, God always answers your prayers. If we are saved and trying to live right with Jesus and trying daily to keep our hearts right with other people, God always answers our prayers.

HOW GOD ANSWERS PRAYERS

Let me tell you the three ways God answers our prayers.

GOD ANSWERS YES TO SOME PRAYERS

One way God answers our prayers is He says "Yes." That's the answer we like, isn't it? James 5:16, says at the end of the verse, "The prayer of a *righteous* man is powerful and effective."

> Elijah was a man just like us. He prayed earnestly that it would not rain, and it did not rain on the land for three and a half years. Again, he prayed, and the heavens gave rain, and the earth produced its crops.
>
> James 5:17-18

Is that not fantastic? Elijah prayed, and God said, "I'm going to give you exactly what you asked for." That is the kind of response I like. Don't you like to pray and get exactly what you asked for? That is one way God answers our prayers. He says yes.

God Answers No to Some Prayers

God also answers by saying no to some of our prayers. Paul tells us he prayed three times for God to answer him regarding an issue (2 Cor. 12). Do you know what happened? God didn't say yes. We forget sometimes, no is an answer.

Have you ever had to say no to your children or grandchildren? Was that an answer? Surely, it was. Sometimes we think yes is the only answer. Every parent who is halfway sane has said no to their children. Every boss has had to say no at some point. No is an answer and, sometimes, God's answer is no.

John Wimber was a charismatic pastor who believed in the power of God healing people, but he was wise enough to know not everyone would be healed. Wimber made a wonderful statement. He said that if you were sick, it was his responsibility to pray for you, and if God chose to say no, God was responsible for that answer. Sometimes the answer to our prayers is no.

Now, if you are praying for someone to be saved, and it has not happened in five years, don't look at that as a no. We are going to see that in that situation you are dealing with a completely different issue. Sometimes, though, when we are praying about things, and God tells us no, we are very happy later that He did. Other times we may not understand this side of heaven why He said no, but no is an answer.

Sometimes God's Answer to our Prayers is Wait

It is really important to understand that sometimes God's answer to our prayers is wait. Zachariah and Elizabeth had prayed for years for a child. They easily could have and probably did believe God was saying no. They probably checked their hearts to see if they were right with God. They were living as they should, but God's answer to them was wait.

They had a son, John. John the Baptist was born at the perfect time because he was Jesus' cousin and lead blocker. John the Baptist came right before Jesus to clear the path for Him. The answer for Zachariah and Elizabeth was wait. When you and I pray, sometimes God's answer to us is wait.

Now, if your twelve-year-old son asks you tonight if he can use the car to cruise around, what will be your response? "No." In one sense it is a no, but that also is a wait. You are going to let him at some point. When he is old enough, you will let him. Sometimes a good parent says wait.

When I first surrendered to preach in 1985, I was dying to pastor. I wanted so bad to pastor, and at seminary they would want me to be a youth minister or to do something else I wasn't called to do. I was called to preach, and they kept trying to put me in other places. I said, "No, I want to pastor."

And God, I thought, kept saying no for a year-and-a-half until finally, finally, I got my own church. I was the happiest guy in the world. God was not saying no to me, God was saying, "Wait. The timing is not right. Your preaching's too bad right now. It'll be bad in six months, but it'll be better." Often what God says to you and me is wait.

You know the cartoon figure, *Ziggy*. One time poor *Ziggy* was praying, looking up to heaven saying, "I feel like I've been on hold with God my whole life." You may be praying about something tonight; you may be on hold.

I'm praying for revival to happen in our church that will turn us upside down, and it has not happened yet. God is not saying, "No." I am sure it is a timing thing. We are just going to keep praying heaven down until it falls on us. God is not saying no there, but He hasn't said yes, yet. Maybe He is waiting for certain things to happen. I don't know. But one answer God gives you and me is wait.

Remember, if you are right with Christ, God always answers your prayers. He hears. He answers. It may be yes, it may be no, it may be wait, but His answer is always what is best.

DOES PRAYING REALLY MATTER?

Does prayer really make a difference? Does praying really matter? You and I have heard people say, "I pray, and nothing happens. I pray, and I am not different. I pray, and my church is not different. I pray, and nothing has changed." We want to know it matters.

I once heard a Christian leader say the people who pray are the ones who believe it makes a difference. But does it? If I'm going to exercise and diet, especially diet, I want to know it is going to make a difference. If you are going to cut four donuts out of my daily routine, I want to know it matters. I want to know it is going to make a difference. Why diet, why exercise, why pray if it doesn't matter?

Some Prayers are Ineffective
Does it make a difference? Let's be honest—for some people, it doesn't. If you are not a Christian, God is waiting for you to enter into that relationship with Him. Does God answer the prayer of the non-Christian for salvation? Absolutely. He is waiting to do that. If

you are not a Christian, your prayers are not going to be effective until you give your life to Christ.

Christian, if you are not right with God or if you have an unforgiving, bitter spirit or sin in your life you are not dealing with, I am going to tell you a hard truth: your prayers do not matter. God is waiting for you to get your act together. The Bible says we do not pray on our terms; we pray on God's terms. We approach prayer on God's terms and what His Word says. I cannot be wrong with God and expect my prayers to make a difference.

SOME PRAYERS MAKE A GREAT DIFFERENCE

If you are right with Christ, your prayers can make a powerful difference. Many people live by this philosophy: we have done everything we can do; I guess we ought to pray now. That makes prayer not our steering wheel but our spare tire, our life preserver. It shouldn't be that way because when you are right with God and you pray, your prayers do make a difference.

James 1:16 says, "The prayer of a righteous man is powerful and effective." God says when you are right with Him your prayers can be powerful and effective.

James says Elijah was a person just like us. He was not a person with a special ability in prayer you can never have. Elijah prayed earnestly that it would not rain, and it didn't rain for three-and-a-half years. Again he prayed and the heavens gave rain, and the earth produced its crops.

Remember if we are going to pray, we have to believe it makes a difference. The Bible says Elijah prayed—it had not rained in three-and-a-half years—and it rained. God was getting ready to destroy millions of people, and Moses begged God not to, and God didn't. David got ready time and time again to go into battle, and God gave the Israelites the victory.

Peter was lying in jail, likely to lose his head the next day. The Christians prayed, the place shook, and Peter walked out of jail. Read your Bible. One thing you will see is prayer can make a difference, and it didn't end in Bible times. Prayer makes a difference today.

In the 1780s, a shoe cobbler named William Carey took a map of the then-known world, and he began to pray, "God, I want to reach the lost people of the world." That began the birth of the modern missionary movement. The Cooperative Program can be traced back to there. Missions began with prayer.

Years ago, a minister was preparing for a great service that thousands of people would be attending. God had so burdened this minister's heart about the service that for twenty-four hours he prayed. And when that service was over, a thousand people were saved.

Charles Mayo, one of the founders of Mayo Clinic, said he had found that when physicians do everything medically possible for people, many times the thing that makes the difference between life and death is prayer. Prayer matters. Prayer makes a difference.

What can your prayers and my prayers do? They can do anything God can do, and God can do everything. When you and I are right with God, our prayers can make an earth-shaking, life-shaking difference. Is that not exciting?

I don't know who said this, but it is worth writing down and remembering. "History will belong to the godly people who will pray." History will be written by godly men and women who pray.

Someday, we are going to get to heaven and find out any success we have had at First Baptist Ruston was a result of our prayers. The revival we believe we are going to have here that will last and last will be a result of prayer. And other people you know that are in heaven, even you yourself, will be there because somebody prayed.

History is being written or not written by prayer or by a lack of prayer. I don't know about you, but I want our church and I want my life to be writing history for God. Prayer makes a difference.

DEDICATE YOUR LIFE TO PRAYER

Christian, are you praying? Prayer is hard work. It takes discipline, but you can do it. Commit yourself to a life of prayer. If you fail in every other adventure in your life but you become a person of prayer, you will die a winner.

Do you want to make your church better? Pray for it. Do you want to make your ministers better? Pray for them. Do you want to make your city better? Pray for it. Do you want to make your family and your world better? Pray for them.

Christian, make a commitment to become a man or woman of prayer. That is what your church needs. That is what your family and your friends need. Maybe you need to say, "I am making this commitment today." Write the date in your Bible and say, "This is going to be a turning point in my prayer life."

I talked with a dear friend in another state about some family members of his who are hard-hearted lost people. He said, "I'm praying for them. That's all I can do." He didn't mean that in a desperate way. He meant, "I tried to talk to them, and they want to cut my head off, but I want to pray for them until they die or I die." He said that because he knows prayer works.

Maybe, Christian, you need to come back to God. Maybe the truth of the matter is your prayers are not effective because of bitterness or sin in your life. Make that right.

Maybe God is saying you need to give your life to Him. Have you never done that? Maybe the reason your prayers have been weak and ineffective through the years is that you have never come to know Jesus. Respond to Jesus, and do what God is leading you to do. First, give your life to Jesus and then give your life to praying to this Jesus who can truly make a difference in your world!

Thank God for the wonderful gift of prayer. Learn to use it.
Show God you love Him by becoming a person of prayer.
God bless. Chris Craig. www.fbcruston.org

Conclusion

I really want to challenge you to become a person of prayer. I know from what the Bible teaches and from personal experience that God uses prayer to change people and to change the world. You and I do not know how much longer we have on this earth, but if you want your time to be well-spent and to matter: become a person of prayer.

God bless you as you enter into or continue on this great journey of communication with God in the days ahead!

Notes

Chapter 1. HOW DO I PRAY

1. R. A. Torrey, *The Power of Prayer,* (Copyright © 1924 by Fleming H. Revell Company, Grand Rapids: Zondervan Books Edition, 1971) 145.
2. Andrew Murray, *With Christ in the School of Prayer* in *Andrew Murray on Prayer*, (New Kensington, PA: Whitaker House, 1998).
3. Charles Stanley, *How to Listen to God*, (Nashville: Thomas Nelson, Inc., 1985).
4. Jerry Rankin, Message, May 1994.

Chapter 2. PRAISING GOD WHEN WE PRAY

1. "Awesome God," Words and Music by Rich Mullins, Nashville: BMG Songs, Inc., 1600 Division St., Suite 225, 1988.
2. Joel C. Gregory, *Growing Pains of the Soul* (Waco: Word Books Publisher, 1987) 26-27.

Chapter 3. IF YOU WANT YOUR PRAYERS ANSWERED, YOU'D BETTER BE RIGHT ON THIS ISSUE

1. Roy Fish, Class Lecture, Southwestern Baptist Theological Seminary, Fall, 1987.
2. William Barclay, *The Daily Study Bible Series*, (The Gospel of Matthew, Vol. 1, Rev. Ed., William Barclay).
3. Corrie ten Boom, *Tramp for the Lord*, (Pennsylvania: Christian Literature Crusade and New Jersey: Fleming H. Revell Company, 1974) 55.

Chapter 4. IF YOU WANT YOUR PRAYERS TO BE HEARD BY GOD, YOU'D BETTER BE RIGHT ON THIS ISSUE, ROUND TWO!

1. Zane Hodges, *The Bible Knowledge Commentary* (An Exposition of the Scriptures by Dallas Seminary Faculty, New Testament Edition, John F. Walvoord and Roy B. Zuck, eds., Wheaton, Illinois: Victor Books, 1984) 886.

Chapter 5. AN IMPORTANT PART OF PRAYING: THANKING GOD

1. Garth Brooks, "Unanswered Prayers," written by Pat Alger, Larry Bastian, and Garth Brooks. CD: No Fences, Release date: 08.27.90. Label: Capitol/EMI Record.
2. "Count Your Blessings," Words by Johnson Oatman, Jr. in *Songs for Young People* by Edwin Excell (Chicago, Illinois: 1897) Music: Edwin O. Excell (MIDI, score).

Chapter 6. THE POWER OF PRAYING FOR OTHER PEOPLE

1. Randolph C. Byrd, M.D., "Positive Therapeutic Effects of Intercessory Prayer in a Coronary Care Unit Population," *Southern Medical Journal*, July, 1988.

Chapter 7. WHAT DOES THE BIBLE SAY ABOUT PRAYING FOR OURSELVES

1. Bruce Wilkinson, *The Prayer of Jabez*, (Sisters, OR: Multnomah Publisher, 2000).
2. John MacArthur, *The Disciples' Prayer* (Chicago: Moody Press Edition, 1986).

Chapter 8. WHAT IS PRAYING IN FAITH ALL ABOUT

1. By Michael A. Fuoco, "W. Va. Celebrates daring rescue of hometown soldier missing in Iraq," *Pittsburg Post-Gazette*, April 01, 2003.

Chapter 9. TO BE EFFECTIVE IN PRAYER, YOU MUST KEEP ON PRAYING

1. Timothy George, *Faithful Witness: The Life and Mission of William Carey*, (Birmingham, AL: New Hope, 1991) 16.
2. Henry Halley, *Halley's Bible Handbook*, 24th ed., Regency Reference Library (Grand Rapids, Zondervan Publishing House, 1965) 516.
3. R. A. Torrey, *Power of Prayer*, (Copyright © 1924 by Fleming H. Revell Company, Grand Rapids: Zondervan Books Edition, 1971) 134-135.
4. Basil Miller, *George Muller, Man of Faith,* (Grand Rapids: Zondervan Publishing House, 1941) 145-146.

Chapter 11. ARE YOU REALLY CONNECTING WITH GOD WHEN YOU PRAY

1. Mark Baggett, "Missionary prayed, robber's pistol misfired," *The Texas Baptist Standard*, 9-1-93.
2. Larry Dossey, MD, by permission. Dossey is author of *Healing Words*, (HarperCollins Publishers, New York, 1993).
3. "National Religious Survey," Barna Associates, cited in *National & International Religion Report*, 3/6/95.

Chapter 12. SOME QUESTIONS COMMONLY ASKED ABOUT PRAYER

1. Phill McHugh, Gloria Gaither and Sandi Patty, "There's Power in the Name of the Lord," River Oaks Music Company/Gaither Music Company/Sandi's Song, 1986.

About the Author

C hris Craig is the senior pastor of First Baptist Church in Ruston, Louisiana. He is married to Cindy, and they have three children: Jason, Julie, and Alicia. Chris and Cindy are also the proud parents of Crunch, a Boxer, and Pebbles, a Rottweiler.

Chris earned his Bachelor of Science Degree from Union University in Jackson, Tennessee. He earned a Master of Divinity from Southwestern Seminary in Fort Worth, Texas, and a Doctor of Ministry Degree from Midwestern Seminary in Kansas City, Missouri. He has been in the ministry for more than twenty years. Chris pastored three churches in Texas before coming to Ruston in January 2003.

Printed in the United States
75158LV00003B/272